In the Forest of Faded Wisdom

Buddhism and Modernity *A series edited by Donald S. Lopez Jr.*

Recent Books in the Series

Critical Terms for the Study of Buddhism, edited by Donald S. Lopez Jr. (2005)

The Madman's Middle Way: Reflections on Reality of the Tibetan Monk Gendun Chopel, by Donald S. Lopez Jr. (2006)

The Holy Land Reborn: Pilgrimage and the Tibetan Reinvention of Buddhist India, by Toni Huber (2008)

Buddhism and Science: A Guide for the Perplexed, by Donald S. Lopez Jr. (2008)

Shots in the Dark: Japan, Zen, and the West, by Shoji Yamada (2009)

In the Forest of Faded Wisdom

104 POEMS by GENDUN CHOPEL

A BILINGUAL EDITION

Edited and Translated by
Donald S. Lopez Jr.

The University of Chicago Press
Chicago and London

Donald S. Lopez Jr. is the Arthur E. Link Distinguished University Professor of Buddhist and Tibetan Studies in the Department of Asian Languages and Cultures at the University of Michigan. His publications include, most recently, *The Madman's Middle Way: Reflections on Reality of the Tibetan Monk Gendun Chopel* (2006) and *Buddhism and Science: A Guide for the Perplexed* (2008), both published by the University of Chicago Press.

The University of Chicago Press, Chicago 60637
The University of Chicago Press, Ltd., London

Printed in the United States of America

18 17 16 15 14 13 12 11 10 09   1 2 3 4 5

ISBN-13: 978-0-226-10452-2 (cloth)
ISBN-10: 0-226-10452-4 (cloth)

The Tibetan portions of the text were typeset by Jo De Baerdemaeker in Lungta, a font that he designed.

Library of Congress Cataloging-in-Publication Data

Dge-'dun-chos-'phel, A-mdo, 1905?–1951?
In the forest of faded wisdom : 104 poems by Gendun Chopel, a bilingual edition / edited and translated by Donald S. Lopez Jr.
p. cm.
Includes bibliographical references and index.
Poems in English and Tibetan.
ISBN-13: 978-0-226-10452-2 (hardcover : alk. paper)
ISBN-10: 0-226-10452-4 (hardcover : alk. paper)
I. Lopez, Donald S., 1952– II. Title.
PL3748.D4A2 2009
985.4.'01—dc22

2008034772

♾ The paper used in this publication meets the minimum requirements of the American National Standard for Information Sciences—Permanence of Paper for Printed Library Materials, ANSI Z39.48-1992.

Contents

Acknowledgments

THE POEMS of Gendun Chopel have never been published in a single volume, and I am grateful to several friends and colleagues for providing me with a number of poems that are not immediately available in his collected works. They include Katia Buffetrille, Isrun Engelhardt, Paul Hackett, Luc Schaedler, Tsering Shakya, Heather Stoddard, and Leonard van der Kuijp. I am grateful to Pema Bhum, director of the Latse Contemporary Tibetan Cultural Library, and his staff for organizing a conference in New York in November 2003 to commemorate the centennial of Gendun Chopel's birth. At this event, several previously unpublished poems were presented. The translation of poetry is a highly interpretative task, and I am grateful to the two readers of the manuscript for the University of Chicago Press, José Cabezón and Lauran Hartley, each of whom offered insightful suggestions for rendering a number of the poems. I would especially like to thank my friend Thupten Jinpa, president of the Institute of Tibetan Classics, who is both a learned scholar of Tibetan poetics and an accomplished poet. Using the miracle of Internet telephony, he discussed each of the poems with me, noting nuances that inevitably elude the nonnative speaker.

Introduction

TIBET has always praised the poet. Over the course of more than a millennium, a sophisticated poetic tradition developed, beginning with songs and laments from the age of its ancient kings, followed by translations of the Sanskrit poems, and Sanskrit poetics, that conveyed so much of Buddhism to Tibet. The various Indian forms did not silence the Tibetan voice; Tibetan poets learned the conventions of Sanskrit poetics and made them their own. Long after the introduction of Buddhism, the voice remained strong in such famous works as the songs of a mountain hermit, the epic recited by bards, and the love poetry of a Dalai Lama.

In recent history, there has been no more famous Tibetan poet than Gendun Chopel (Dge 'dun chos 'phel, 1903–1951). He attracted acclamation and excoriation over the course of his short and controversial life. But both his devoted advocates and his bitter adversaries agreed on one thing: he was a consummate poet. In a culture where poetry is considered the highest form of human language, Gendun Chopel is revered as Tibet's greatest modern poet. He was a master of the many forms of Tibetan verse: the ancient lyric, the classical Indian *kāvya*, the "alphabetical poem," the song of religious experience. He is known as well for what are regarded as technical skills: his wordplay, his puns, his ability to evoke moods of pathos and of irony. His vocabulary was vast, as was his knowledge of Buddhism and of Tibetan history; he enriched his poetry with allusions conveyed by a single word, sometimes adopting an archaic spelling to conjure an earlier age. He was a master craftsman of Tibetan verse, but there is also a spontaneity about his poetry. As a young monk visiting a powerful lama, Gendun Chopel presented him with a painting, then turned it over to pen a four-line poem that incorporated the syllables of the lama's name.

Gendun Chopel wrote poetry throughout his life, and much of his verse is autobiographical. One of the hallmarks of his work is the immediacy with which he conveys the events of his remarkable life, sometimes caustically, sometimes poignantly. It is therefore perhaps useful to begin with a brief account of his life, interspersed with passages from his poems.

He was born in Amdo, the northeastern region of the Tibetan culture domain. His father was a tantric priest of the Nyingma or "ancient" sect of Tibetan Buddhism, which traces its roots to the highly mythologized visit to Tibet of the Indian master Padmasambhava at the end of the eighth century. Padmasambhava is said to have hidden many texts in the mountains, lakes, and valleys of Tibet so that they might be discovered in subsequent centuries. These texts, called treasures (*gter ma*) in Tibetan, are a central constituent of the vast Nyingma canon. Gendun Chopel's father was an accomplished scholar of a genre of this literature called the Heart Essence of the Great Expanse (*Klong chen snying thig*).

The early decades of the twentieth century were a period of vibrant religious activity in Amdo, in the midst of which Gendun Chopel seems to have been regarded as a prodigy; at the age of five he was recognized as the incarnation of the abbot of a famous Nyingma monastery. His father taught him spelling, grammar, and poetry, beginning at the age of three. He also learned many prayers by heart. His studies continued after his father's death, when the boy was six years old. At age eight, he studied (in Tibetan translation) the standard handbook on Sanskrit poetry, the *Mirror of Poetry* (*Kāvyādarśā*), composed in the seventh century by Daṇḍin. At age twelve, he wrote a poem in perhaps the most challenging of forms, an auspicious circle (*kun bzang 'khor lo*). In one version, a grid of squares, eighteen by eighteen, is drawn, and a syllable is placed in each square such that the syllables can be read as a poem in multiple directions. Gendun Chopel is said to have written two of these poems when he was twelve. Only one such poem by him survives (poem 15), where he writes:

Refined subtle essence purified by fire,
A body where infinite light-forms converge as one.
You are teacher, the taught, the audience.

It is unclear whether this is one of his youthful works; that it is dedicated to a famous Nyingma lama (Gter bdag gling pa, 1646–1714) suggests that it could be.

Around the age of twelve, he entered a local Geluk monastery, where he distinguished himself in his studies. The Nyingma and Geluk sects are often portrayed as bitter rivals. That Gendun Chopel, the child of a Nyingma family, would enter the Geluk academy, apparently with his late father's blessing, suggests that this storied rivalry may not have been so strong, at least at this time and in this place. Gendun Chopel would excel in the Geluk curriculum but never lost sight of his family traditions, which recur throughout his poems. His Nyingma filiation, however, would eventually come to haunt his legacy.

After several years at the small Geluk monastery and some instructions in tantric meditation from a Nyingma lama, he moved (sometime between 1920 and 1923) to the great monastery of Labrang, one of the six great Geluk monasteries of Tibet, having some four thousand monks. There he continued to excel in his studies, especially in the ritualized debate for which the Geluk are so famous. He gained particular notoriety as a debater who could hold, and successfully defend, unorthodox positions. And he continued to write poetry. One poem that survives from this period is his prayer to the goddess Sarasvatī, the patron of scholars and poets (poem 16). He writes:

May you adorn my throat
With words to clarify the world.

Gendun Chopel is said to have been critical of philosophical positions set forth in the monastery's textbooks. Although his skill as a debater certainly delighted some, it angered others, and he came to be labeled as a *tha snyad pa*, a term that he would come to use to refer to himself in his poetry. It is a difficult term to translate, with meanings ranging from "lover of words," to "rhetorician," to "sophist." In this last sense, it refers to someone who is skilled in words but has little appreciation or interest in their deeper meaning. It was in this sense that it was used by his antagonists at Labrang. This reputation was at least one of the reasons that Gendun Chopel left the monastery in 1926. He departed bitterly and wrote a poem (poem 31) about the experience, describing himself as a simple and studious monk banished from the monastery, while all manner of immoral monks were permitted to stay:

Rather than banishing to distant mountain passes, valleys, and towns
Those who take pride in studying the books of Ra and Se
Would it not be better to banish to another place
Those proudly selling meat, beer, and tobacco?

Nonetheless, he seems to have remained close to some of the monks at the monastery, sending poems back to them during his time in India (for example, poem 64). First, however, he returned home, where he read the songs of the great nineteenth-century Nyingma yogin Shabkar (Zhabs dkar tshogs drug rang grol, 1781–1851). His reading moved him to compose a poem of praise (poem 17), where he writes:

Abiding at a lofty stage, all treatises on logic
Were perfected long ago in wondrous ways,
Appearing without obstruction
In the mirror of your clear mind.

In 1927, not quite twenty-four years old, Gendun Chopel bade farewell to his mother, his sister, and his village, never to return. Accompanied by an uncle and a cousin, he joined a caravan for the four-month trek to Lhasa, the capital of Tibet. There he entered Drepung, one of the "three seats" of the Geluk sect in Lhasa and the largest monastery in the world, having at that time some eleven thousand monks. He resumed his studies, again gaining a reputation as a skilled debater. As before, he was known as something of a contrarian, falling into shouting matches with his teacher, the distinguished scholar (and skilled poet) Sherab Gyatso (Shes rab rgya mtsho, 1884–1968), who eventually refused to address Gendun Chopel by name, calling him simply "the madman." He continued to write poetry during this period, but also developed as a painter, and supported himself by selling his works. At Drepung Monastery, he lived at a college called One Hundred Thousand Dragons with other monks from his home region of Amdo. Several years after his arrival, his cousin was killed in an accident. Gendun Chopel wrote a poem about his death (poem 33), which contains these lines:

Dear childhood friend, radiant half of my heart,
When the flower of youth blossomed,
The streams of our minds mixed.
Where in the six realms could you be now?

In 1934, the Indian scholar and patriot Rahul Sankrityayan (1893–1963) arrived in Lhasa in search of Sanskrit manuscripts, especially those dealing with Buddhist logic. He needed a guide to lead him to the great libraries of the monasteries of southern Tibet, and to negotiate with the abbots for permission to explore their often musty contents. He enlisted Gendun Chopel for the task, just as he was completing the final examinations at the end of the long curriculum of the Geluk geshe. After their bibliographic tour had concluded, Pundit Rahul, as he was called, invited Gendun Chopel to return with him to India. Gendun Chopel accepted the invitation. Leaving Lhasa in 1934, he would not return until 1946.

He traveled extensively, and often alone, across India and Sri Lanka, learning Sanskrit, Pāli, and several Indian vernaculars as well as English. As he writes in a poem he sent back to the monks at Labrang (poem 64):

With the years of my youth passing away
I have wandered all across the land of India, east and west.
I have studied Sanskrit, most useful,
And the useless language of the foreigners.

Gendun Chopel gained an intimate knowledge of Sanskrit poetry by translating into Tibetan Kālidāsa's classic play, *Śakuntalā,* several chapters of the *Bhagavad Gītā,* and portions of the Hindu epic the *Rāmāyaṇa,* and he read the devotional poetry of Tulsīdās. He is also said to have translated Daṇḍin's *Mirror of Poetry* from Sanskrit into Tibetan, although this work was lost. He assisted the Russian Tibetologist George Roerich in the translation of the important, and unreadable, fifteenth-century history of Tibetan Buddhism, the *Blue Annals* (*Deb ther sngon po*). This was tedious and difficult work, and Gendun Chopel did not feel that his contributions to the project were properly acknowledged by Roerich (poem 32):

The talents of a humble scholar, seeking only knowledge
Are crushed by the tyranny of a fool, bent by the weight of his wealth.
The proper order is upside down.
How sad, the lion made servant to the dog.

While in Kalimpong, he assisted the French scholar Jacques Bacot in the translation of several Dunhuang manuscripts from the Tibetan dynastic period. In these pages he read songs of the ancient Tibetan kings; these songs would inspire some of the poems in his unfinished history of early Tibet, the *White Annals* (*Deb ther dkar po*). His study of these annals occurred during a vibrant period in the Indian independence movement, one that Gendun Chopel witnessed firsthand. His poems about the ancient Tibetan empire are filled with martial imagery and a welling sense of patriotism; the following is from poem 82:

It is said that Tibet's army of red-faced demons,
Pledging their lives with growing courage

To the command of the wrathful Hayagrīva,
Once conquered two-thirds of the earth's circle.

He visited and made studies of most of the important Buddhist archaeological sites in India, writing a guidebook that is still used by Tibetan pilgrims today. And he studied Sanskrit erotica and frequented Calcutta brothels, producing his famous sex manual, the *Treatise on Passion* (*'Dod pa'i bstan bcos*), written entirely in verse. He explains, for example (poem 90):

Because men and women are so different,
If they were not joined by coupling,
The world would be split into two factions
Always in quarrels and war.

Before undertaking his research, Gendun Chopel renounced his monastic vows, including the vow of celibacy. Such a decision is traditionally traumatic for a Tibetan monk, and he alludes to it on several occasions in his poetry.

During his time abroad, he spent more than a year in Sri Lanka, at that time the British colony of Ceylon. This was his only extended stay in a Buddhist country other than Tibet, and his observations are fascinating. Accompanying the monks on their begging rounds, he writes, "I thought, 'I alone am seeing this legacy of our compassionate teacher.' On many occasions, my eyes filled with tears and I had to sit on the ground for a moment." In a poem about his time in Sri Lanka (poem 38), he observes:

Although the dress of a monk has long disappeared
And the practice of monastic discipline has left no trace,
This meeting with the assembly of elder monks
Must be the fruit of a deed in a former life.

Also while there, he translated the classic early Buddhist poem, the *Dhammapada*, from Pāli into Tibetan.

Gendun Chopel lived for twelve years abroad and would not live long after his return to Tibet. It was in India and Sri Lanka that he would compose his famous works (with one exception) and write his most famous poems. His longest—and in his view his most important—work is *The Golden Chronicle, the Story of a Cosmopolitan's Pilgrimage* (*Rgyal khams rig pas bskor ba'i gtam rgyud gser gyi thang ma*), which he wrote between 1934 and 1941. Over six hundred pages in length, it details what he learned during his early years in South Asia, about India and Sri Lanka as well as Tibet. It contains his translation of the rock edicts of the Buddhist emperor Aśoka; the first sustained Tibetan discussion of Western science; and discussions of Hinduism, Jainism, Sikhism, Islam, and Theosophy, along with a scathing critique of European colonialism. It begins and ends with long poems, and most of its seventeen chapters contain at least one four-line poem. This is one example (poem 39):

Not acting as a real cause of heaven or liberation,
Not serving as a gateway for gathering gold and silver,
These points that abide in the in-between,
Cast aside by everyone, these I have analyzed in detail.

This brief poem contains themes that appear frequently in the poetry written by Gendun Chopel while abroad. Although he was a highly trained scholar of Nyingma and Geluk, and widely and deeply read in the vast literature of Tibetan Buddhism of all sects, he was not regarded as a lama and did not write traditional Buddhist treatises. Thus, what he wrote did not produce the benefits of a traditional Buddhist teaching; it was not a "real cause of heaven," that is, an auspicious rebirth or "liberation," the achievement of buddhahood. In both his prose and his poetry, he is also a keen, and cynical, observer of hypocrisy, contemptuous especially of those who, in the guise of Buddhist teachers, gather great wealth for themselves. Living at the edge of poverty in India, he is certainly not such a person. His writing, therefore, also does not serve "as a gateway for gathering gold and silver." Instead, he takes a certain pride in investigating what lies between God and Mammon, those topics that neither the pious nor the pecuniary pursue. The term translated as "the in-between" is the Tibetan term *bar do*, made famous by the so-called *Tibetan Book of the Dead* in describing the netherworld between one lifetime and the next.

Like a person living in the liminal world of the *bar do*, Gendun Chopel often portrayed himself as someone alone and forgotten. Although he sometimes traveled with a companion (unacknowledged), he also spent many days traveling alone, a destitute foreigner unfamiliar with the local language. Indeed, the word *unfamiliar* (*rgyus med*) appears often in his poetry. In Tibetan, it connotes that of which one has no knowledge, no experience, although there is something more visceral about the word in Tibetan. Gendun Chopel also wrote often of being lost in a foreign land; the Tibetan term he used, *mi yul*, can also mean "land of humans." His sense of being alone was only heightened by his fear that he had been forgotten at home. With a mixture of despair and resentment, he worried that what he had written, sent to "unseen friends," would not be read—or if read, would not be appreciated. His long poem at the end of *The Golden Chronicle* (poem 42) begins:

> Walking with weary feet to the plains of the sandy south,
> Traversing the boundary of a land surrounded by the pit of dark seas,
> Pulling the thread of my life—precious and cherished—across a sword's sharp blade,
> Consuming long years and months of hardship, I have somehow finished this book.
>
> Although there is no one to beseech me
> With mandates from on high or maṇḍalas of gold,
> I have taken on the burden of hardship alone and written this,
> Concerned that the treasury of knowledge will be lost.

His fears of oblivion were not entirely unfounded. Gendun Chopel's collected works, including *The Golden Chronicle* and many of his poems, were not published until 1990, almost four decades after his death. During his lifetime, some works, such as his guidebook to India, were published; others, like his *Treatise on Passion*, circulated in manuscript form; many of his poems were simply memorized by those who heard them and transmitted orally. The printing press had not been introduced into Tibet when he was writing in India; books were still printed from hand-carved woodblocks, a process that required resources or a patron, neither of which he possessed.

Gendun Chopel's primary venue for his poems and essays during his years abroad was the only Tibetan-language newspaper of the day. Called *Melong* (its English name was the *Tibet Mirror*), it was founded in 1925 by the Tibetan Christian Dorje Tharchin (Rdo rje mthar phyin, 1890–1976). It was published not in Lhasa, but in Kalimpong in northern India, in the borderland between Nepal, Sikkim, and Bhutan. It was in *Melong* in 1938 that Gendun Chopel published his famous essay in which he argues that the world is round. Some of his articles about the origins of Tibetan orthography appeared there. Several of his alphabetical poems (including poems 54 and 79) were also published there. He even wrote a poem in praise of the Christian virtues of his friend Dorje Tharchin, which Tharchin, editor of the paper, printed on the front page (poem 61).

Gendun Chopel also wrote poems in English during his years abroad, and some of these were published in the *Maha-Bodhi*, the journal of the Maha Bodhi Society, which had been founded in 1891 by the Buddhist modernist

Anagārika Dharmapāla. The circumstances under which he wrote these poems, composed in a rather florid style, are unknown, but it seems likely that he received some assistance. Here is an unpublished example (poem 100), written in a childlike style in his own hand in 1943.

Look at God by two small eyes
Listen to him by two small ears
Serve him by two small hands
Go to the church by two small feet
Tell the truth by a small tongue
Be loved by a small heart
Praise God for ever and pray to him.

Yet two years earlier, in 1941, he had published a poem in the *Maha-Bodhi* about Lake Manasarowar, written in unrhymed trochaic tetrameter, immediately recalling *The Song of Hiawatha*. Here is one stanza (poem 101):

The young hunter aims his arrow,
And, behold, he sees thy water,
And no more sees he the roebuck
Slacks the bowstring, flees the quarry.

The identity of Gendun Chopel's collaborator is unknown; he is said to have worked with an unidentified Roman Catholic nun on the translation (now lost) of the *Commentary on Valid Knowledge* (*Pramāṇavārttika*), Dharmakīrti's famous seventh-century treatise, written in verse, on Buddhist logic and epistemology. And he had been befriended by the American Tibetophile Theos Bernard, the self-proclaimed "white lama," who had invited him to come to the United States, an invitation he was prevented from accepting by the outbreak of World War II.

In January 1946, after twelve years abroad, Gendun Chopel returned to Lhasa. He soon gathered a circle of friends around him—some old acquaintances from his days in the monastery, others young, forward-thinking lamas and aristocrats—to whom he taught poetry, illustrated by verses of his translation of *Śakuntalā*. He also gave teachings on Madhyamaka philosophy, which would be published posthumously as the *Adornment for Nāgārjuna's Thought* (*Klu sgrub dgongs rgyan*). Although written in prose, the work contains a number of poems, two of which are particularly famous. The first is the obeisance to the Buddha with which the book begins (poem 26):

To the sharp weapons of the demons, you offered delicate flowers in return.
When the enraged Devadatta pushed down a boulder, you practiced silence.
Son of the Śākyas, incapable of casting even an angry glance at your enemy,
What intelligent person would honor you as a friend for protection from the great enemy, fearful saṃsāra?

The poem begins with a reference to the famous attack by Māra, the Buddhist god of death and desire, against the Buddha on the night of his enlightenment. The hail of weapons unleashed by Māra and his host of demons was transformed into a shower of blossoms. Later, in a struggle for succession, the Buddha's evil cousin, Devadatta, attempted to assassinate the Buddha by rolling down a great boulder to crush him. But the boulder merely grazed the Buddha's toe. In the face of his enemies, indeed, of those seeking his death, the Buddha responded with a patient silence. A more traditional paean to the Buddha would ask, "What intelligent person would not honor you as a friend for protection from the great enemy, fearful saṃsāra?" That is, the Buddha is the safest place of refuge from the sufferings of the cycle of rebirth, and thus it is appropriate that he be so honored. Gendun Chopel, however, turns this sentiment on its head, asking, "What intelligent person would honor you as a friend for protection from the great enemy, fearful saṃsāra?" That is, what person in his or her right mind would seek protection in someone who would not even defend himself? Gendun Chopel's implication, of course, is that the true Buddhist is not in his or her right mind; that the teachings of the Buddha completely undercut what the world regards as sanity. In this regard, Gendun Chopel was proud to be a madman.

The other famous poem in the *Adornment for Nāgārjuna's Thought*, one that he may have composed before returning to Tibet, is a critique of what the world regards as sanity, or in the terminology of Buddhist philosophy, conventional valid knowledge (*tha snyad tshad ma*). This poem (poem 28) is filled with the technical vocabulary of Buddhist scholasticism, but its point is simple:

Here in the capital of six types of beings who cannot agree,
What is asserted by ten is not asserted by a hundred;
What is seen by humans is not seen by gods.
Who makes the laws that validate truth and falsity?

Within a few months of his arrival in Lhasa, Gendun Chopel was arrested by the government of the young Dalai Lama. The formal, and fabricated, charge was counterfeiting foreign currency. The true reasons remain unknown; it is known that the British counsel in Lhasa had warned the Tibetan government of Gendun Chopel's dangerous political views. After repeated questioning in the city jail, questioning that included flogging, he was transferred to the main prison at Zhol at the foot of the Potala, the Dalai Lama's winter palace. Sentenced to three years, he served at least two. He was given paper and pen in his cell and continued to write, working on his history of ancient Tibet and also writing poems. A beautiful poem (poem 1), evoking imagery of the pre-Buddhist religion of Tibet, was written from prison. When Gendun Chopel was finally released, poem 58 was said to have been found written on the mattress in his cell:

In the jungle where the frightful roar resounds
Of the stubborn tiger drunk on the blood of envy,
The honest little child is left all alone.
May the wise think of him with compassion.

The regent of Tibet, ruling during the Dalai Lama's minority, was named Daktrak Rinpoche (Stag brag rin po che, 1874–1952), whose name means "tiger rock."

Gendun Chopel had acquired the vices of smoking and drinking while in India, and after his release from prison he seems to have descended into alcoholism. He abandoned his various projects and rarely displayed flashes of his former brilliance. He looked back on his life in two short poems (poems 52 and 51); the precise dates of composition are uncertain.

In my youth, I did not take a delightful bride;
In old age, I did not amass the needed wealth.
That the life of this beggar ends with his pen,
This is what makes me feel so sad.

The other poem (poem 51) is said to have been recited spontaneously by Gendun Chopel at some point after his return to Tibet, when one of his students asked him to compose a biography in verse:

A virtuous family, the lineage of monks, the way of a layman,
A time of abundance, a time of poverty,

The best of monks, the worst of laymen,
My body has changed so much in one lifetime.

The word translated as "family" is *gdung* in Tibetan, literally *bone,* a term used in the sense of *blood* in English to refer to a family over several generations. Here it can refer to Gendun Chopel's natal family—he came from a long line of tantric priests—as well as to the line of his previous incarnations. Born into this family, he then received ordination as a Buddhist monk and entered the lineage of the Buddha. Either shortly before or soon after his departure for India, he renounced his monk's vows to become a layman.

An impoverished layman, recently released from prison, his body ravaged by cirrhosis of the liver as he watched the People's Liberation Army enter Lhasa, the greatest Tibetan poet of the twentieth century died on October 12 (or 14 or 15), 1951. As he lay dying, he asked that two poems be read to him, one by the Geluk master Tsong kha pa (1357–1419), the other by the Nyingma master Mi pham (1846–1912).

THE POEMS

In a modern Tibetan encyclopedia, the entry "Poetry" (*snyan ngag*) begins with this sentence: "In general, poetry is said to be the melodious and euphonious use of words in order to provide imagery for the myriad ways that life in the worldly realm appears to the human mind." Poetry in Tibet is considered something to be vocalized and listened to rather than written and read. The various names for the ancient forms of Tibetan verse, the *gur* (*mgur*), the *shay* (*gzhas*), and the *lu* (*glu*), all might be translated into English as "song." The Tibetan translation of the Sanskrit term *kāvya* literally means "melodious speech" (*snyan ngag*).

The evolution of Tibetan poetry might be divided into three phases. The first would be the pre-Buddhist phase. Writing was not introduced into Tibet until the introduction of Buddhism there in the seventh century, but many songs of the ancient kings seem to have been preserved orally; some of these appear in the manuscripts discovered in the library cave at Dunhuang. The subject matter of these songs ranges widely; it includes extravagant boasts about oneself and one's clan, disparaging challenges to one's foes, love songs and laments, riddles, and verses on various pastoral themes. These poems were composed of verses, each only five or six syllables in length, with the same sound often doubled (and sometimes tripled) at the end of the line.

The second period would be the early Buddhist phase, marked by the invention of the Tibetan alphabet; the translation of Buddhist texts, many of them in verse, from Sanskrit into Tibetan; and the journeys to India by Tibetans to study with tantric masters, who introduced them to the various genres of tantric songs, the *dohā* and the *gīti*, said to be spontaneous expressions of the realizations of the great adepts. The songs of Milarepa (1040–1123), disciple of Marpa the Translator (1012–1097) who himself went to India three times, are the most famous poems of this period.

The third phase of Tibetan poetry is marked by the introduction of Daṇḍin's seventh-century handbook on Sanskrit poetics, the *Mirror of Poetry* (*Kāvyādarśa*). The Sanskrit term *kāvya* means "that which comes from a *kavi*," a term that can mean a wise man, a seer, a prophet, a sage, a bard. Thus, *kāvya* can mean "poetry," but it is usually translated into English as "ornate poetry" or "court poetry," because it is so stylized. However, Daṇḍin makes it clear that *kāvya* need not be in verse; it can include poetry, prose, and works that mix the two. *Kāvya* is characterized by elaborate metaphors and similes; obscure terms, grammatical forms, and allusions; compounds that can be read to yield multiple, and even contradictory, meanings; internal rhyme schemes; and the use of a variety of meters.

Daṇḍin's text is perhaps the most famous of many Indian works on poetics. It is concerned especially with rhetorical embellishments or adornments (*alaṃkāra*). These include similes (of which he enumerates thirty-two types), hyperbole, and double meanings, as well as various types of rhymes and repetitions of sounds and letters. For each of these, Daṇḍin gives examples, usually of his own composition. He provides, for instance, twenty-five ways to compare a beautiful face to a lotus flower.

The *Mirror of Poetry* was introduced into Tibet in the thirteenth century by the great scholar Sakya Paṇḍita (1182–1251) when he included extended excerpts from it in his *Entrance Gate for the Learned* (*Mkhas pa rnams la 'jug pa'i sgo*). Daṇḍin's text was translated into Tibetan in full shortly thereafter, and then repeatedly over the centuries. Gendun Chopel especially praised the translation by Si tu Paṇ chen (1699–1774), although he apparently also translated it himself. Many texts on Sanskrit poetics were eventually translated into Tibetan, but Daṇḍin's work remained the fundamental treatise for Tibetan poetics, and Daṇḍin was widely regarded as the greatest Sanskrit poet (although Gendun Chopel preferred Kālidāsa). One was not considered highly educated if one had not studied the *Mirror of Poetry*, and even the most sober monks sought and gave instruction on it. A common exercise in erudition was to compose examples of the various poetic forms that Daṇḍin enumerates; Gendun Chopel is said to have done so at the age of eight. This is not to suggest that Sanskrit poetic figures displaced all forms of earlier

Tibetan verse. It is the case, however, that after the thirteenth century, learned Tibetan conceptions of poetry were reshaped.

For example, from this point onward the basic unit of the Tibetan poem was the four-line stanza, the Tibetan version of the Sanskrit *śloka*. In Sanskrit, the *śloka* was composed of thirty-two syllables, commonly in two lines of an equal number of syllables. Each line was divided into two feet (*pāda*), also of an equal number of syllables; feet were often of eight syllables, lines of sixteen. In rendering Sanskrit verse into Tibetan, the translators gave a full line to each of the four feet; thus, what was two lines in Sanskrit would be rendered as four in Tibetan. Each of the four lines was of an equal number of syllables, most commonly seven and sometimes nine.

Tibetan words contain syllables, each of which is separated by a dot in the written form. Each syllable carries some meaning, either as a word in itself or as a grammatical marker. Words usually have two syllables, the first of which is accented. Some of the ancient Tibetan songs are composed of lines of six syllables each, but in the Buddhist period the lines are most often of an odd number, as noted usually seven or nine but as long as twenty-three. The standard meter was trochaic. The odd number of syllables in each line provided Tibetan poets with two advantages. First, it allowed them to end the thought expressed by the line or to continue it to the next; to achieve this effect the poet could employ either a full stop or a continuative marker, respectively. The odd number of syllables also preserved the oral quality of Tibetan verse. Raising the voice on the last syllable cued the listener to extend the thought to the next verse; lowering the voice on the last syllable indicated that the thought was complete. Although in Sanskrit verse the two-line stanza was regarded as a self-contained unit, Tibetan poets sometimes employed the odd-numbered line to extend a thought over several stanzas.

Within this basic structure, Tibetan poets crafted their own embellishments, such as starting each line with the same syllable, repeating the same syllable in each line, or using a single vowel sound in all syllables of a line. Tibetan personal names typically contain four syllables, and in writing verses in honor of a particular person it was common to use each of the four syllables of the name in each line of the stanza. Tibetan poets also employed all manner of puns and onomatopoeia. A form that was considered a particular display of poetic prowess was the *ka rtsom* or *ka bshad*, which might be translated as "alphabetical poem." The Tibetan alphabet has thirty letters, and the challenge presented by this form was to write a thirty-line poem, with each line beginning with a letter of the alphabet, in the proper sequence. It was not sufficient to start the line with a word that began with that letter; the letter had to stand alone. This was possible because each Tibetan letter also has a meaning, either as a single syllable or as part of a two-syllable word. Thus, *kha,* the second letter, means "mouth"; *nga,* the fourth letter, means "I"; *nya,* the eighth letter, means "fish"; *tsha,* the eighteenth letter, means "hot"; *sha,* the twenty-seventh letter, means "meat." The challenge, then, was to compose a long poem that made sense from line to line using each of the thirty letters. The best poets tried to eschew the letters' common meanings for something more arcane. The problem was that for the less commonly occurring letters in the Tibetan alphabet, the choices were highly limited. The twentieth and most rarely used letter, *wa,* means "fox." As a result, foxes are frequent inhabitants of the alphabetical poem.

Gendun Chopel was the master of all these forms, composing poems that displayed a high level of technical skill but that remained at once elegant and earthy. (Poems 31, 53, 54, 61, 74, and 79 are all alphabetical poems, something that unfortunately cannot be duplicated in translation.) He most often wrote nine-syllable verses, but ranged from as short as seven or eight to as long as eleven or fifteen. As an example of his wordplay, one might consider the following excerpt from poem 5:

shar nub rgya mtsho'i mtha' la thug gi bar
lho phyogs rgya gar yul du bgrod pa'i tshul
nub kyi smag la sgron me bteg 'dra 'di
byang phyogs bod kyi skyes bu'i don du 'bri

rgya khyon mtsho dang 'dra ba'i grong khyer dang
rgya 'phang ri dang 'dra ba'i mchod rten sogs
rgya che'i gzigs mo mang po gzigs pa'i slad
rgya gar yul du lan gcig 'byon par mdzod

Each line is nine syllables in length. Each of the first four lines begins with one of the four cardinal directions: East (*shar*), South (*lho*), West (*nub*), North (*byang*). Each of the next four lines begins with the same syllable: *rgya* (pronounced *gya*), meaning "broad" or "vast." All of this, sadly, is lost in translation:

This way to travel to the land of India in the south
Reaching to the ends of the oceans of the east and west,
This lamp raised in the darkness of the west
Was written for the people of Tibet in the north.

The cities like vast oceans,
The stūpas like vast mountains,

To see so many vast sights
Come but once to this vast land of India.

Gendun Chopel was also fond of using numbers in his poems, with the numbers one, two, three, and four appearing in each of the four lines of the stanza. In poem 5, he extends the number to eight, making good use of the various lists that abound in Buddhism.

Gendun Chopel was not only a poet but a teacher of poetry, and had clear ideas about the training of a poet. For example, he felt that the aspiring poet should begin by writing poems of seven-syllable lines before moving to longer lines. Longer lines are, in fact, easier to compose, but if one begins with those, it is harder to move to the shorter lines. He also believed that it was difficult to compose authentic poetry in a foreign language. He wrote some poems in English and felt that he developed a certain level of taste, but also thought that they sounded unnatural. He explained to a friend that if one was not familiar with a language from one's youth, it was very difficult to write good poetry in that language. Among the many Mongolians who wrote Tibetan poetry, he judged that only one could write poems that sounded as if they had been composed by a native speaker of Tibetan.

THIS BOOK

For this volume I have translated all the poems of Gendun Chopel that I have been able to locate. Most of these have been published; a few have not. During his years abroad, Gendun Chopel sent poems back to Tibet; some of these continue to be discovered. When he returned to Lhasa in 1946, he brought with him a large metal box that contained the works he had composed during his travels. The box was confiscated upon his arrest, and its fate remains a mystery. Thus, I cannot claim that this book contains all of the poems that Gendun Chopel had written. We can only hope that more will be discovered.

Among his published poetry, two important works, or groups of works, have been omitted. He translated a number of Sanskrit works, such as chapters of the *Bhagavad Gītā*, into Tibetan. These were in Sanskrit verse, and he rendered them in Tibetan verse. These are not included. Second, his famous work on erotica, the *Treatise on Passion* (*'Dod pa'i bstan bcos*), is written entirely in verse. Since it has already been translated, albeit largely in prose (by Jeffrey Hopkins as *Tibetan Arts of Love*), I have provided only a few excerpts from that work here.

Gendun Chopel did not gather his poems into a single volume, nor have they been gathered in Tibetan since his death in 1951; the largest group (thirty poems) was published in Tibet in 2005 in volume 5 of his collected writings, in a chapter entitled "On Poetry" (*Snyan rtsom gyi skor*). Several dozen additional poems are found throughout the five-volume collection, in such works as the *Golden Chronicle*, the *Adornment for Nāgārjuna's Thought*, and the *White Annals*. More poems had appeared earlier, in a volume of newly discovered writings of Gendun Chopel, published in Tibet in 2002. And at a conference celebrating the centenary of his birth in 2003, held at the Latse Contemporary Tibetan Cultural Library in New York, photocopies of three previously unknown poems were distributed to the audience.

Some of the poems have titles; most do not. In the case of poems that have been published in more than one book, the same poem will sometimes have different titles, with the title in some cases simply being a line of that poem. Since it is unclear which, if any, of these titles were provided by the author, with the exception of the English poems, no titles have been given to the poems translated here (although they are provided in the notes); for the sake of reference, they have been randomly numbered. Gendun Chopel was not averse to self-citation, and the same stanzas, sometimes with minor variation, are to be found among his poems. When the poem is a single stanza that also appears as part of a longer work, I have translated the longer work and not provided a separate and additional translation of the shared stanza. It is also the case that parts of various poems have been combined into a single poem, apparently by an editor. I have not translated these poems, following for the most part the versions that appear in an earlier three-volume edition of his collected works, published in 1990 and edited by his friend and disciple Hor khang.

The circumstances of composition and the composition date of a given poem are rarely known. For each poem I have provided a note indicating the Tibetan source, the existence of any duplicate or variant versions of the poem, and whatever might be known about when, for whom, and why it might have been written.

Gendun Chopel's poems are presented here in five sections, organized, rather crudely, by theme. The first section is entitled "Teachings of a Master without Disciples." As noted above, Gendun Chopel was a highly trained Buddhist scholar. While a child he had been identified as the incarnation of a Nyingma lama, and he had been trained at the highest levels of the Geluk academy. He was among the most erudite Buddhist scholars of the twentieth century. He thus wrote many poems with Buddhist themes, many of which contain instructions on how to practice the Buddhist path. But, as he often lamented, he wrote without being empowered to do so by a high lama or at the request of a powerful patron. Nor was he approached by students who offered him gold in exchange for his teachings. This did not prevent him from writing beautiful Buddhist poetry, but, like so many of his works, he did so wondering whether it would ever be read.

Echoing this theme, the next section is entitled "Laments of an Unknown Sage." The poems included here are the most autobiographical, beginning with the poem Gendun Chopel wrote after leaving Labrang Monastery. He felt misunderstood and unappreciated throughout his life, feelings that were only magnified by the long years spent wandering in strange lands far from home. These are the most personal of the poems, sometimes caustic, sometimes melancholy.

The third section, "The Ways of the World," features those poems that in one way or another provide the trenchant observations of someone who believed that he had seen it all. He was clearly an astute student of human nature, and in these poems the world-weary traveler describes, often with a certain cynicism, the people and places he has encountered. His recreations of a classical Indian style also appear here.

The fourth section is entitled "Songs of the Tibetan Kings." For the most part, the poems in this section are associated with the *White Annals*, Gendun Chopel's unfinished history of the ancient Tibetan empire. The tone and the vocabulary are quite different here. He often seeks to evoke a Tibet prior to the introduction of Buddhism, employing terms and themes that he found in the Dunhuang manuscripts. These are the poems of a Tibetan patriot, proud of his people and their warlike ways.

The fifth section, "Precepts on Passion," contains excerpts from his erotic handbook, the *Treatise on Passion* (*'Dod pa'i bstan bcos*). Here I have attempted to provide selections that give a sense of the range of this fascinating text, including both specific instructions in the arts of love as well as more philosophical passages on the nature of passion.

These five headings are admittedly imperfect, and a single poem could easily be placed in a different section of this book. Buddhist themes and terms pervade almost all the poems, and cynical observations about human greed are often paired with passages on the Buddha's infinite compassion. For Gendun Chopel, orgasm was the common person's path to bliss, such that even the instructions on lovemaking are also intimations of esoteric tantric teachings. And there was rarely a circumstance in which Gendun Chopel was reluctant to proclaim his own learning or decry his sad state. Following these five sections are the few English poems.

Gendun Chopel has become an iconic figure—both in Tibet and in the Tibetan exile community—since his death in 1951. And like many icons, his name is evoked more often than his words are read. The purpose, or at least the hope, of this volume is that Gendun Chopel's most beautiful words, his poetry, will be read by the audience they deserve. On the left-hand pages, those who can read Tibetan will find his poems in their original language. On the right-hand pages, those who cannot read Tibetan will find my imperfect, though heartfelt, renderings of his poems into English.

FURTHER READINGS ON TIBETAN POETRY

Stephan V. Beyer, *The Classical Tibetan Language*. Albany: State University of New York Press, 1992.

José I. Cabezón and Roger Jackson, eds., *Tibetan Literature: Studies in Genre*. Ithaca, NY: Snow Lion Publications, 1995.

Thupten Jinpa and Jaś Elsner, *Songs of Spiritual Experience: Tibetan Buddhist Poems of Insight and Awakening*. Boston: Shambhala, 2000.

Victoria Sujata, *Tibetan Songs of Realization: Echoes from a Seventeenth-Century Scholar and Siddha in Amdo*. Leiden: E. J. Brill, 2005.

Teachings of a Master without Disciples

. ༡ .

འདི་ན་སུ་དང་གང་གིས་སྨྲ་ཤེས་པའི། །
གཡུང་དྲུང་ལྷ་ཡི་རྒྱ་ཐག་རིང་མོ་འདིས། །
མཐའ་མེད་ཆོས་དབྱིངས་རིག་པའི་དབྱིངས་སུ་བཏགས། །
རིག་པའི་བྱ་ཆུང་ལུས་ཀྱི་ནང་དུ་བཏགས། །
ལུས་ཀྱི་ཐོ་ཡོར་ཟས་དང་སྨན་ལ་བཏགས། །
ཟས་དང་སྨན་ནི་ཕྱི་རོལ་རྒྱུན་ལ་བཏགས། །
དེ་ལྟར་ཐག་པ་གཅིག་ལ་གཅིག་འཐུད་པ། །
གཅོད་པའི་ས་མཚམས་གཞན་ནི་ཡོད་མ་ཡིན། །

ས་མཚམས་གཅིག་ནི་ཀུན་གྱིས་སྨྲ་འདོད་པ། །
ལུས་སེམས་འབྲེལ་ཐག་ཆོད་པའི་འཆི་བ་ཉིད། །
ས་མཚམས་གཅིག་ནི་ཀུན་གྱིས་སྨྲ་ཤེས་པ། །
ཐག་པ་ཙལ་ནས་དབྱིངས་རིག་འདྲེས་པ་ཉིད། །

སེམས་འདི་མཐའ་དང་བྲལ་བའི་ལྷ་མོ་སྟེ། །
ལྷ་མོའི་ཕ་ཡུལ་འཛིག་རྟེན་འདི་མིན་མོད། །
སེམས་ཀྱི་ལྷ་མོའི་ཞབས་ཀྱི་མཐེ་ཆུང་གཅིག།
སྐྱུད་པས་ལུས་པོ་འདི་ལ་དམ་དུ་བཏགས། །

དེ་ནས་སྐྱུད་པ་འདི་ཉིད་ཆད་ཀྱི་བར། །
ལུས་ཀྱིས་གང་སྤྱོད་སེམས་ཀྱིས་སྤྱོད་པར་སྣང་། །
མཐེ་ཆུང་འདི་ལ་ཕན་གནོད་གང་བྱས་པས། །
ལྷ་མོ་དེ་ལ་བདེ་སྡུག་སྤྱོད་པར་ཟད། །

ཐག་པ་འདི་དེ་ཆད་ན་ལེགས་མོད་ཀྱང་། །
ཐག་པ་ཆད་པར་འཛིག་རྟེན་ཐམས་ཅད་སྐྲགས། །
ཐག་པས་འབྲེལ་བའི་ཐབས་ལ་འབད་པ་ནའ། །
ཐག་པའི་སྣེ་ཀུན་ཆོར་མས་དཀྲིས་པར་མཐོང་། །

ཆོར་མའི་རྩེ་མོ་རེ་རེ་འགོག་སླད་དུ། །
ཤེས་རིག་ལས་ཀྱི་རྣམ་གྲངས་རེ་རེ་བསླབ། །

. 1 .

Unknown here by anyone in any way
This long cord of the changeless god
Ties the boundless sphere of reality to the sphere of awareness
Ties the awareness of the child to the interior of the body
Ties the stone heap of the body to food and drink
Ties food and drink to external causes.
Thus the cord is tied, one to the other.
There are no points where it can be cut but these:

The first place is desired by none;
It is death, where the cord of body and mind is cut.
The other place is known by none;
It is where the cord decays, merging sphere and mind.

This mind is a goddess, beyond all bounds.
The homeland of this goddess is not this world,
Yet the little toe of the goddess of the mind
Is tied tightly to this body by a thread.

Then, until this thread is cut
Whatever the body feels, seems to be felt by the mind.
Whatever help or harm is done to this little toe
The goddess feels as pleasure and pain.

If the cord is cut, all is well.
Yet the whole world fears the cord's cutting.
In striving to keep the cord connected
The ends of the cord become wrapped in thorns.

To extract the point of each thorn
We study each category of culture;

དེས་ན་ཆོར་མ་འགོག་པའི་ཁྲལ་ལས་འདི། །
མ་ཤིའི་བར་དུ་བྲེལ་བས་ཕྱེད་པར་ཟད། །

ཚར་མེད་སྤྲང་དུ་མེད་པའི་བྲེལ་བ་འདི། །
ཀུནད་ཀྱི་སྐྱེ་བ་བླངས་པའི་དོན་སྙོར་སྣང་། །
མཁའ་དང་མཉམ་པའི་སེམས་ཀྱི་ཆ་ཤས་གཅིག།
ཤ་ཁྲག་ལས་ཀྱི་འདམ་དུ་ཚུད་པ་ནའ། །
ཚ་གྲང་བགྲེས་སྐོམ་རེ་དོགས་འཇིགས་སྐྲག་གི།
སྡུག་བསྔལ་འདི་ལ་ཟད་མཐའ་སྨྱེད་པ་སྣམ། །

འོན་ཀྱང་འབད་པ་བརྒྱ་ཡིས་སྒྲུབ་སྒྲུབ་པའི། །
ཤེས་རིག་དཔལ་གྱིས་བསྐྲུན་པའི་ལུས་པོ་འདི། །
ཆོས་ཉིད་གནམ་གྱི་རྒྱལ་མོའི་བཀའ་ལུང་བཞིན། །
ས་སྟེང་འདི་རུ་ལོ་ཤས་སྡོད་པར་ཟད། །

མགུར་འདི་སྐད་ཅེས་བླངས་སོ། །

. ༢ .

དུས་གསུམ་རྒྱལ་བ་ཀུན་གྱི་ཕྲིན་ལས་གཟུགས། །
ཐར་འདོད་སྐྱེ་རྒུ་ཡོངས་ཀྱི་དཔུང་དང་གཉེན། །
ཉམ་ཐག་འགྲོ་བ་ཀུན་ལ་བརྩེ་བའི་མ། །
རྗེ་བཙུན་སྒྲོལ་མའི་ཞབས་ལ་གསོལ་བ་འདེབས། །

གཡུ་མདོག་ལང་ཚོ་དར་བ་མཛེས་པའི་སྐུ། །
སྲིད་ཞིའི་གདུང་བ་ཀུན་སེལ་སྙན་པའི་གསུང་། །
སྒྲིབ་གཉིས་གྲིབ་མ་རྣམ་དག་སྙིང་རྗེའི་ཐུགས། །
རྗེ་བཙུན་སྒྲོལ་མའི་ཞབས་ལ་གསོལ་བ་འདེབས། །

རྒྱུས་མེད་ཡུལ་དུ་ལམ་སྟོན་ས་མཁན་མཛད། །
འཇིགས་པའི་འཕྲང་དུ་སྐྱོབས་པའི་སྐྱེལ་མ་གནང་། །
དབུལ་ཞིང་ཕོངས་ཚེ་མཁོ་བའི་ལོངས་སྤྱོད་སྩོལ། །
རྗེ་བཙུན་སྒྲོལ་མའི་ཞབས་ལ་གསོལ་བ་འདེབས། །

We stay busy with this taxing toil,
Extracting thorns until we die.

This unfinished busyness, never abandoned,
Seems an entrance; its purpose the rebirth of beings.
When just one part of this mind, equal to space,
Sinks into the mire of deeds of flesh and blood,
Then come terrors of hot and cold, hunger and thirst, hope and fear.
I wonder if this suffering ever ends.

Yet this body, fashioned by the glory of culture,
Achieved through a hundred endeavors,
In keeping with the truth of the queen of heaven's prophecy
Must remain on this earth a few more years.

I sang this song.[1]

. 2 .

Your form, the deeds of all the victors of the three times;
Friend to the host of beings seeking liberation;
Mother who loves all miserable migrators.
I pray at the feet of lady Tārā.

Your beautiful body, the color of turquoise, restores health;
Your sweet speech dispels the longing for existence and peace;
Your compassionate mind purifies the stains of the two obstructions.
I pray at the feet of lady Tārā.

You serve as a guide, showing me the path in an unknown land;
You serve as an escort, protecting me on a frightening precipice;
You grant the resources I need when I'm impoverished.
I pray at the feet of lady Tārā.[2]

. ༣ .

གང་ལ་བརྟེན་ན་བསླུ་བ་མ་མཆིས་པའི། །
སྐྱབས་གནས་རིན་ཆེན་གསུམ་གྱི་ཐུགས་རྗེའི་མཐུས། །
དོན་མེད་འཁོར་བའི་འཕྲུལ་སྣང་ཀུན་ཞི་ནས། །
བློ་སྣ་ཆོས་ལ་ཕྱོགས་པར་བྱིན་གྱིས་རློབས། །

ཅི་ལ་བསམས་ཀྱང་འཇིག་རྟེན་བྱ་གཞག་ལ། །
ཡང་སྙོམས་སྙིང་པོ་ཏིལ་ཙམ་མི་འདུག་པས། །
ཡུན་ཐུང་ཚེ་འདིའི་བློ་སྣ་བསྒྱུར་བྱས་ཏེ། །
ད་ནས་སྙིང་པོའི་ལྷ་ཆོས་བྱེད་པར་བྱ། །

དར་མའི་ན་ཚོད་དབྱར་གྱི་མེ་ཏོག་ཙམ། །
མཛེས་པའི་བཀྲག་མདངས་དགུན་གྱི་འཇའ་ཚོན་ཙམ། །
མི་ཡི་ཚེ་ལ་ཡུན་ལོང་མི་འདུག་པས། །
ད་ནི་སྙིང་པོའི་ལྷ་ཆོས་བྱེད་པར་བྱ། །

སྡུག་པའི་དུས་སུ་སྐྱིད་པའི་ཐབས་ལ་རེ། །
སྐྱིད་པའི་དུས་སུ་སྡུག་བསྔལ་ཡོང་གིས་དོགས། །
རེ་དོགས་འཕྲང་ལས་ཐར་དུས་མི་འདུག་པས། །
ད་ནི་སྙིང་པོའི་ལྷ་ཆོས་བྱེད་པར་བྱ། །

གཅེས་པར་བསྐྱངས་ཀྱང་ནད་དང་གཙོང་གི་གཞི། །
རྒྱན་གྱིས་མཛེས་ཀྱང་མི་གཙང་རང་བཞིན་ཉིད། །
མི་རྟག་ལུས་ལ་སྙིང་པོ་མི་འདུག་པས། །
ད་ནི་སྙིང་པོའི་ལྷ་ཆོས་བྱེད་པར་བྱ། །

ཕྱུག་པོ་ཕྱུག་པོའི་ས་ནས་སྡུག་གཏམ་བྱེད། །
དབུལ་པོ་དབུལ་པོའི་ས་ནས་སྨྲེ་ངག་འདོན། །
མི་རེའི་སེམས་ལ་སྡུག་བསྔལ་ཁུར་པོ་རེ། །
འཁོར་བའི་གནས་ན་བདེ་བའི་སྐབས་མ་མཆིས། །

སྤྱིར་ན་ཕྱི་རོལ་བདེ་སྡུག་སྣང་བ་ཀུན། །
རང་གི་སེམས་ཉིད་གཅིག་པོའི་ཆོ་འཕྲུལ་ཏེ། །

. 3 .

Compassionate power of the three jewels,
Reliable refuge that never deceives,
Calming all illusions of meaningless saṃsāra
Bless our minds to turn to the dharma.

Whatever we ponder, the affairs of the world
Have no more essence than a sesame seed;
Transform our minds in this short life;
Starting now, reveal the essential sacred dharma.

The time of youth is but a summer flower
The luster of beauty but a winter rainbow.
Since human life does not last long
Practice the essential sacred dharma now.

In times of sorrow, we hope for joy.
In times of joy, we fear the coming sorrow.
There is no time free from the straits of hope and fear;
Practice the essential sacred dharma now.

Cherished and protected; base of sickness and disease,
Made elegant with ornaments; its nature is impurity.
The impermanent body has no essence.
Practice the essential sacred dharma now.

The rich complain from the place of the rich.
The poor weep from the place of the poor.
Each human mind has its own burden of suffering;
There is no happy time in saṃsāra.

In general, all joys and sorrows that seem outside
Are magical creations of one's mind alone;

ནང་གི་གཟུགས་བརྙན་ཕྱི་རུ་འཆར་བ་ལས། །
ཕྱི་ཡི་རྣམ་པ་ཚུར་ལ་འོངས་པ་མིན། །

དེ་ལྟར་ལེགས་པར་གོ་ནས་དཔྱད་པ་ཡིས། །
ཀུན་གཞི་སེམས་ཀྱི་རྩ་བ་ཆོད་པའི་ཚེ། །
སྣང་བའི་ན་བུན་འདི་ཡི་ཕ་རོལ་ན། །
ཆོས་ཉིད་དོན་གྱི་ནམ་མཁའ་དངོས་སུ་བཞུགས། །

ཡོད་ཅེས་བྱ་བ་འདི་ཡང་བཅོས་མ་སྟེ། །
མེད་ཅེས་བྱ་བ་འདི་ཡང་བཅོས་མ་ཉིད། །
དེ་འདྲའི་བཅོས་མ་ཀུན་གྱིས་མ་བསླད་པ། །
སེམས་ཀྱི་རང་བཞིན་རྫོགས་པའི་སངས་རྒྱས་ཡིན། །

ཡིན་མིན་རྣམ་རྟོག་ཆུ་ཡི་གཉེར་མ་བཞིན། །
གཅིག་རྗེས་གཅིག་གིས་མཐུད་དེ་འགྲོ་བ་འདི། །
གཏོད་མེད་དང་དུ་ལྷོད་ཀྱིས་ཞིགས་པའི་ཚེ། །
ཆོས་དབྱིངས་གདོད་མའི་རྒྱ་མཚོར་སླེབས་པ་ལགས། །

མདོར་ན་སྣང་བ་སེམས་ཀྱི་ཆོ་འཕྲུལ་ཏེ། །
སེམས་ནི་སྟོང་པ་གཞི་མེད་རྩ་བྲལ་ཉིད། །
གཞི་མེད་ཆོས་ལ་བདག་ཏུ་བཟུང་བ་ཡིས། །
ཁྱོད་དང་ང་ཡང་འཁོར་བའི་གནས་སུ་འཁྱམས། །

དེ་ནི་སྣང་བའི་རྗེས་སུ་མ་འབྲང་བར། །
སྣང་མཁན་ཁོ་ལ་ཅེར་གྱིས་བལྟས་པའི་ཚེ། །
བརྗོད་དུ་མེད་པའི་རང་ངོ་མཐོང་འགྱུར་བས། །
སངས་རྒྱས་ཐོབ་པའི་ལམ་དེ་ཐག་མི་རིང་། །

དེ་ལྟར་རྩ་གསུམ་ལྷ་ཡི་བྱིན་རླབས་ཀྱིས། །
མྱུར་དུ་རང་སེམས་སྟོང་པའི་རྩད་ཆོད་དེ། །
ཀ་དག་རྫོགས་པ་ཆེན་པོའི་རྒྱལ་ས་ནས། །
མཐའ་མེད་འགྲོ་བའི་དོན་ཆེན་བྱེད་པར་ཤོག།

Reflections from inside that appear outside,
Not things outside that have come near.

Knowing this well, when analysis
Severs the root of the basic mind,
You will abide in the true sky of reality
Beyond this fog of appearance.

This so-called existence is a fiction.
This so-called nonexistence is a fiction.
Untainted by all such fictions,
The nature of the mind is perfect buddhahood.

Thoughts of "is" and "is not" are like ripples in water;
They follow one after the other.
Dissolving easily into the aimless state,
They arrive at the ocean of the primordial sphere of reality.

Appearances are the magical display of the mind.
The mind is empty, without base, without foundation.
By holding baseless phenomena to be the self
You and I wander in the realm of saṃsāra.

Without pursuing perceptions,
When you look directly at the perceiver itself,
You will see your own inexpressible face;
The path to achieve buddhahood is not far.

Through the blessings of the divine three foundations,
May you quickly find the emptiness of your own mind,
And from the kingdom of the ever-pure great perfection,
Bring about the great aims of boundless beings.[3]

. ༨ .

དྲི་མེད་ཐེག་པ་ཆེན་པོའི་ཐེམ་སྐས་ལས། །
འོད་གསལ་སེམས་ཀྱི་བང་རིམ་འཛེགས་པ་ཡི། །
འོག་མིན་ཆོས་ཀྱི་ཁྲི་ལ་དབང་བསྒྱུར་བའི། །
རྣམ་འདྲེན་དོན་ཀུན་གྲུབ་པས་དགེ་ལེགས་སྩོལ། །

. ༩ .

ཉག་ཅིག་ཞི་བའི་དབྱིངས་སུ་འཇུག་པའི་སྒོ། །
བདེན་གཉིས་ཆོས་ཚུལ་ཟབ་མོ་དྲི་མེད་ལམ། །
རིགས་གསུམ་གདུལ་བྱའི་ཚོགས་ལ་སྟོན་མཛད་པའི། །
སྐུ་བཞིའི་བདག་ཉིད་སངས་རྒྱས་དེ་ལ་འདུད། །

རྒྱུད་ལྷས་བསྐུས་པའི་འགྲོ་བ་མ་ལུས་པ། །
ཕྱིན་དྲུག་ཕ་རོལ་ཕྱིན་པའི་ལམ་བརྟེན་ཏེ། །
ནོར་བདུན་ཡོན་ཏན་ཚང་བའི་རྟེན་བརྒྱུད་ནས། །
མཐའ་བརྒྱད་སྤྲོས་པ་དག་པའི་སྐུ་ཐོབ་ཤོག།

ཤར་ནུབ་རྒྱ་མཚོའི་མཐའ་ལ་ཐུག་གི་བར། །
ལྷོ་ཕྱོགས་རྒྱ་གར་ཡུལ་དུ་བགྲོད་པའི་ཚུལ། །
ནུབ་ཀྱི་སྐག་ལ་སྒྲོན་མེ་བཏེག་འདྲ་འདི། །
བྱང་ཕྱོགས་བོད་ཀྱི་སྐྱེས་བུའི་དོན་དུ་འབྲི། །

རྒྱ་ཁྱོན་མཚོ་དང་འདྲ་བའི་གྲོང་ཁྱེར་དང་། །
རྒྱ་འཕང་རི་དང་འདྲ་བའི་མཆོད་རྟེན་སོགས། །
རྒྱ་ཆེའི་གཟིགས་མོ་མང་པོ་གཟིགས་པའི་སྐད། །
རྒྱ་གར་ཡུལ་དུ་ལན་གཅིག་འབྱོན་པར་མཛོད། །

. 4 .

Ruling on the dharma throne of Akaniṣṭa,
Ascended by the steps of the mind of clear light
From the staircase of the stainless great vehicle,
May the guide who achieves all aims bestow good fortune.[4]

. 5 .

The one door of entry into the realm of peace is
The two truths: profound doctrine, stainless path.
You reveal this to the assembly of disciples of the three lineages.
I bow to you, the Buddha, four-bodied lord.

All beings included in the five lineages
Depend on the path of the six perfections.
Relying constantly on all the qualities of the seven jewels
May they attain the body free of the eight extremes of elaboration.

This way to travel to the land of India in the south
Reaching to the ends of the oceans of the east and west,
This lamp raised in the darkness of the west
Was written for the people of Tibet in the north.

The cities like vast oceans,
The stūpas like vast mountains,
To see so many vast sights
Come but once to this vast land of India.[5]

. ༦ .

གཅིག་གཅིག་གཉིས་སུ་མེད་པའི་དམ་པའི་ཆོས། །
གཉིས་གཉིས་བཞི་ཡི་བདེན་པའི་དོན་རྟོགས་ཏེ། །
གསུམ་གསུམ་དྲུག་གི་ཕ་རོལ་ཕྱིན་པའི་ལམ། །
བཞི་བཞི་བརྒྱད་ཀྱི་མཐའ་རྣམས་དེ་ལ་འདུས། །

. ༧ .

མ་ཆགས་པདྨའི་སྤྱན་ལྡན་ལྷ་མིའི་གཉེན། །
སྲིད་པས་མཆོད་འོས་བསོད་ནམས་སྟོང་གི་སྐུ། །
ཤིན་ཏུ་རྣམ་དག་གསེར་གྱི་འོད་མདངའ་བ། །
མཉན་ཡོད་བཞུགས་པ་དེ་ལ་ཕྱག་འཚལ་ལོ། །

གང་དུ་བདག་གི་སྟོན་པ་སྐུ་འཁྲུངས་ཤིང་། །
གང་དུ་འདྲེན་པས་བྱང་ཆུབ་མཆོག་བརྙེས་ཏེ། །
འཆི་མེད་ལམ་བསྟན་མྱ་ངན་འདས་པ་ཡི། །
རྒྱ་གར་གནས་ཆེན་རྣམས་ལ་ཕྱག་འཚལ་ལོ། །

. ༨ .

ཐོག་མ་མེད་ནས་ཧག་ཏུ་འགྲོགས་པ་ཡི། །
མི་འགྱུར་སེམས་ཀྱི་གཤིས་ཀྱང་མི་མཐོང་ན། །
བཙན་ཐབས་སྒྲོམ་གྱིས་གསར་དུ་བསྐྲིད་པ་ཡི། །
ཡ་མཚན་གྲུབ་པའི་གཟིགས་སྣང་ག་ལ་མཐོང་། །

. 6 .

One plus one, the true dharma that is not two.
Two plus two, realizing the meaning of the four truths.
Three plus three, the path of six perfections.
Four plus four, the eight extremes included in that.[6]

. 7 .

To the friend of gods and humans, with lotus eyes of nonattachment,
A body made of thousands of virtuous deeds, worthy of the world's worship,
Endowed with the color of the purest gold,
To the one who abides in Śrāvastī, I bow down.

Where my teacher was born,
Where the guide found supreme enlightenment,
Where he taught the path to the deathless state and then passed beyond sorrow,
To the great holy sites of India, I bow down.[7]

. 8 .

If the unchanging nature of the mind is not seen
Though it has been with you always without beginning,
How can you see wondrous visions
Newly created through forceful meditation?[8]

. ༩ .

སྙིང་རྒྱས་རི་བོའི་ནགས་སུ་བཙོམ་ལྡན་འདས། །
མཉམ་བཞག་གཡོ་མེད་དཀྱིལ་མོ་ཀྲུང་མཛད་དེ། །
གང་ཞིག་གཟིགས་པའི་ཟབ་མོའི་བདེན་པ་དེ། །
མ་ལུས་འགྲོ་ལ་མངོན་དུ་འགྱུར་བར་ཤོག།

གོ་འཕང་གང་ཞིག་ཁམས་གསུམ་སྐྱེ་རྒུ་འདིའི། །
ཚིག་དང་བློ་དང་དཔྱོད་པའི་ཡུལ་མིན་པ། །
གང་དུ་བདེ་བར་གཤེགས་པ་གཤེགས་གྱུར་པའི། །
ཞི་བའི་ས་དེ་མྱུར་དུ་རྙེད་པར་ཤོག།

. ༡༠ .

དྭངས་བསལ་ཆུ་རིས་འཁྲིགས་པའི་སྨིག་རྒྱུའི་མཚོ། །
ཐྲན་བྲལ་བྱེ་མའི་ཐང་དུ་ངོ་འཕྲོད་དེ། །
མི་འདོད་དངོས་པོ་བདེན་དུ་སོང་བ་འདི། །
འཁོར་བས་བསླུས་པའི་སྡུག་བསྔལ་ཆ་ཤས་ཙམ། །

. ༡༡ .

ཕྱོག་གྱུར་དོན་ལ་གཞོལ་བའི་མི་མཐུན་ལུང་། །
བདེན་པའི་དབྱེ་བ་འབྱེད་པའི་ང་རྒྱལ་གྱིས། །
རྩོད་པའི་ཐལ་མོ་ཕན་ཚུན་བསྣུན་པ་འདི། །
རིགས་པའི་རྒྱལ་བོའི་བསྟན་ལ་མཛེས་མ་ཡིན། །

. 9 .

The Bhagavan sat cross-legged in unmoving equipoise
In the forest on a broad-topped mountain.
May the profound truth that he saw
Become manifest to all migrators.

That state is not an object of words, minds, or analysis
By these creatures of three realms.
May the state of peace where the Sugata has gone
Be swiftly found.[9]

. 10 .

The mirage of a lake of clear water with patterns of waves
Is recognized to be a plain of dry sand.
Unwanted things that come to be true
Are but portions of the suffering gathered in saṃsāra.[10]

. 11 .

Striking the palms together in debate
Proudly making distinctions in the truth
Found in conflicting scriptures on obscure topics;
This does not adorn the king of reasoning's teaching.[11]

· ༡༢ ·

མཁས་པས་རྒྱལ་ཁམས་འགྲིམ་སྐྱེ་བསགས་བྱས་པའི། །
དབུལ་པོའི་གཅེས་ནོར་ས་ལ་བཀྲམ་པ་འདི། །
སྙན་ནས་སྙན་དུ་ཤུབ་བུར་བརྒྱུད་པ་ཡི། །
ཕྱུག་པོའི་གསེར་ཆོས་དག་གིས་དོ་ཟླ་མིན། །

· ༡༣ ·

ཐབས་ཤེས་གོམས་པའི་མངོན་རྟགས་སུ། །
བཟོ་བོ་རང་གིས་ལེགས་བྲིས་པའི། །
ཞབས་མཐིལ་འཁོར་ལོའི་རི་མོ་དེས། །
སྐྱེ་དགུ་འདི་དག་སྲུང་གྱུར་ཅིག།

· ༡༤ ·

སྲིད་པའི་ཐ་སྙད་ལམ་ནས་སྲིད་པའི་འགྲོ། །
སྲིད་ལས་འདས་པའི་དབྱིངས་སུ་འཁྲིད་མཛད་པ། །
སྲིད་གསུམ་འགྲོ་བའི་ས་མཁན་ཆོས་ཀྱི་རྗེ། །
སྲིད་ཞིའི་རྣམ་འདྲེན་རྡོ་རྗེ་གདན་པར་འདུད། །

རྒྱ་ཆེན་རྒྱལ་ཁམས་ཀུན་གྱི་རིགས་པའི་དབྱིག།
མི་འཇིགས་དུས་བཞིའི་མཐར་ཡང་བསྲུང་བའི་སླད། །
གངས་རིས་བསྐོར་བའི་མཛོད་དུ་ལེགས་བསྡུས་པའི། །
སྔོན་བྱོན་ལོ་པཎ་དེ་དག་ཕྱག་གི་ཡུལ། །

. 12 .

Spread upon the ground, this pauper's precious treasure,
Gathered by a scholar as he wandered through the realms,
Is no match for the rich man's golden dharma,
Passed down in whispers from ear to ear.[12]

. 13 .

May the wheels on the soles of his feet,
Drawn well by the artist himself,
Marks of his mastery of method and wisdom,
Protect all these creatures.[13]

. 14 .

Leading worldly beings from the path of worldly conventions
To the sphere beyond the world,
Lord of the dharma, guide for beings of the three worlds,
I bow down to the leader of existence and peace, the Holder of the
Diamond Throne.

Objects of veneration are the paṇḍitas and translators of the past
Who gathered well into a treasury ringed by snowy mountains
The jewels of knowledge of all vast realms
To safeguard them even to the end of four ages.[14]

སྐུ་གསུམ་རྒྱལ་བའི་ཡེ་ཤེས་དྭངས་མའི་ཁམས། །
འདབ་སྟོང་པད་མའི་ལྦུམས་སུ་འཁྲིལ་བ་ལས། །
ངོ་མཚར་སྤྲུལ་པའི་གཟུགས་སུ་ལེགས་བལྟམས་པ། །
རྒྱལ་དབང་མཚོ་སྐྱེས་རྡོ་རྗེས་དུས་ཀུན་སྐྱོངས། །

གང་གི་གྲགས་པའི་འབྲུག་སྟོང་སྒྲ་ཡིས་རྣམ་པར་ལྡིར་བའི་ས་ཆེན་གཞིར། །
དྲེགས་པའི་ཁྱད་སྙེགས་ཅིག་ཅར་འགྱེལ་བའི་རྒྱལ་ཕྲན་ཀུན་གྱི་རལ་པ་ལ། །
མ་བྲིས་འཁོར་ལོའི་གཙུག་རྒྱན་བཀོད་པས་ལེགས་བྲིས་རིན་ཆེན་སྐྱེངས་བྱས་པ། །
ཟུར་གསུམ་འཛམ་གླིང་འཛིན་མའི་དབང་ཕྱུག་མངའ་བདག་རྒྱལ་པོ་རྒྱལ་གྱུར་ཅིག།

ཚུལ་ཁྲིམས་དད་ལྡང་དམར་སེར་བླ་གོས་ཀྱིས། །
ཁ་བའི་སྨ་ཕྲེད་གསེར་གྱི་ཁ་དོག་ཏུ། །
སྒྱུར་བའི་བྱེད་པོ་བྱང་ཆུབ་སེམས་དཔའ་ཡི། །
བཀའ་དྲིན་མི་ཤེས་དཔྱོད་ལྡན་སུ་ཞིག་ཡོད། །

ཐུགས་རྗེའི་བདུད་རྩིའི་ཆར་གྱིས་བརླན་པས་རིགས་གསུམ་སྐལ་བཟང་དགའ་བ་བསྐྱེད། །
མཐུ་སྟོབས་གནམ་ལྕགས་ཐོག་གིས་བསྡིགས་པས་སྲིད་གསུམ་དྲེགས་པའི་སྙིང་རྩ་འདར། །
ཆོས་ཟད་ཀློང་ནང་ཆོས་ཀུན་གཟིགས་པས་དུས་གསུམ་རྒྱལ་བ་དགྱེས་བཞད་མཛད། །
སྨོས་རིགས་ལྷ་ཡི་ཞབས་ཀྱི་པད་མོ་སྒོ་གསུམ་དང་བས་སྤྱི་བོར་བསྟེན། །

. 15 .

The refined element of the wisdom of the triple-bodied victors,
Settling in the womb of a thousand-petaled lotus,
Was wellborn in the form of a wondrous emanation.
O king of victors, Lotus-born Vajra, care for me at all times.

In this great earth, thundering with the sound of a thousand dragons proclaiming his fame,
The well-drawn gems increased, placed in the crown of the undrawn circle of his locks.
In all the small kingdoms, the footstools of arrogance were simultaneously toppled.
May you rule as lord, master, and king of the earth, three-cornered Jambudvīpa.

What discerning person does not know the kindness
Of the bodhisattva who transformed
The Ring of Snows into a golden color,
Whose orange robe spread the scent of ethics?

Moistened by the rain of the ambrosia of compassion, the good fortune and joy of the three lineages grow.
Threatened by the powerful thunderbolt, the hearts of the demons of the three realms tremble.
Seeing all phenomena within the expanse that is the extinction of phenomena, the victors of the three times smile with delight.
With the three doors pure, I keep the lotus feet of the Nyö clan's god at the crown of my head.

[*At this point the poem shifts to the grid form described in the introduction.*]

སེམས	ཉིད	གདོད	ནས	དག	པའི	ནམ	འགྱུར	ལ	འགག	མེད	རིགས	ལྔའི	འཇའ	འོད	འཁྲིགས	པ	ཉིད
རྡོ	རྗེ	སློབ	དཔོན	གཟུགས	སྐུ	རབ	ཤར	བ	སྐུ	གསུམ	མངའ	བདག	གྲུབ	པའི	དབང	པོ	རྒྱལ
རྒྱུས	མེད	རྡོ	ལ	གནས	པའི	རིན	ཆེན	བཞིན	འགྱུར	མེད	རིག	པའི	རང	བཞིན	ངོ	སྤྲོད	པའི
རྩོད	མེད	རྟག	བརྟན	རྡོ	རྗེ	སྙིང	པོའི	དོན	གྲངས	མེད	མཁས	པ	ཀུན	གྱི	དབུས	སུ	གྲགས
གནས	གསུམ	མཁའ	འགྲོས	རྟག	ཏུ	མཆོད	ཕྱས	ཞིང	སྲིད	གསུམ	འཇིག	རྟེན	ཀུན	ལ	ཡོངས	གྲགས	པའི
བཅུ	གསུམ	གྲངས	ལྡན	འཁྲུལ	མེད	སྙིང	པའི	གཙོ	ས	གསུམ	མགོན	པོ	གཏེར	བདག	གླིང	བ	རྒྱལ
སྐྱེས	པའི	དགའ	པ	བཅུ	དྲུག	འགྱུར	བ	ཅན	སྐྱེ	མེད	དངོས	པོའི	གཤིས	དང	འདྲེས	པ	ལས
རྡོ	རྗེ	ཐུགས	ཀྱིས	བརྟན	གཡོ	ཀུན	ཁྱབ	པ	བསམ	ཡས	ཆོས	ཀྱི	སྐུ	མངའ	ཕྲིན	ལ	འདུད
བཙོ	བསྒྲིགས	སྦྲངས	པའི	ཕྲ	མོའི	དངས	མ	ཀུན	མཐའ	མེད	འོད	ལུས	གཅིག	ཏུ	འཁྲིལ	བའི	སྐུ
འཆད	པོ	ཆོས	ཀྱང	རང	སྡེ	འཁོར	ཀྱང	རང	ཅིར	ཡང	ཡོངས	སྤྱོད	རྫོགས	པ	ཕྲིན	ལ	འདུད
རྟོགས	བྲལ	ཆ	ལ	ཆ	ཟླ	ཧི	བཞིན	ཏུ	སྣར	ཡང	འགྲོ	བ	དུག	གི	ཁམས	རྣམས	སུ
མ	ངེས	སྤྲུལ	པའི	ཐུགས	རྗེའི	འོད	སྙིང	ཅན	རྣམ	ཀུན	འཆར	བ	ཕྲིན	ལ	གུས	པས	འདུད
ཐེག	དགུའི	ཡང	རྩེ	འོད	གསལ	རྫོགས	ཆེན	བསྟན	གདངས	རིའི	ར	བ	ཁྱབ	པའི	རིན	ཆེན	གདུགས
བཤད	སྒྲུབ	ས	ཡི	སྙིང	པོའི	ཡུ	བ	ཡིས	འབུམ	ཕྲག	སྐལ	བཟང	དཔལ	དུ	འདེགས	པར	མཛོད
མཆོ	སྐྱེས	རྗེ	རྗེའི	ཐུགས	བཅུད	གསང	བའི	མཛོད	མི	ཤིགས	བཀའ	རྒྱ	བདུན	ལྡན	གཏེར	གྱི	སྒོ
ཡེ	ཤེས	སྐྱེ	མའི	འཕྲུལ	གྱིས	ལེགས	ཕྱེས	པའི	ངོ	མཚར	གྲགས	པ	སྲིད	པའི	གླུ	ན	འབར
རྣམ	འཕྲུལ	སྣ	ཚོགས	ཐབས	མཁས	སྒྲོ	བརྒྱ	ཡིས	སྙིགས	མ	ལྔ	བརྒྱའི	དུས	ཀྱི	མཐའ	མར	ཡང
གར	དབང	པད	མའི	རིང	ལུགས	སྤེལ	མཛད	པ	གྲུབ	བརྒྱའི	གཙུག	རྒྱན	གཏེར	བདག	གླིང	པར	འདུད

Upon the transformations of mind itself, primordially pure,
The rainbow of unimpeded five-colored light gathers.
Appearing in the form of a vajrạ master,
O lord of adepts, endowed with the three bodies, may you be victorious.

Like a jewel abiding unknown within a stone,
The undisputed, eternal essence of the vajra
Points out the nature of unchanging awareness,
This is renowned to countless scholars.

Always worshipped by ḍākiṇīs of the three abodes,
Chief of the unmistaken Ling-pa who number thirteen
Renowned throughout the threefold world,
O Ter-dak ling-pa, protector of the three realms, may you be victorious.

By fusing the sixteen joys, born and changing
With the nature of things, unborn,
You pervade the entire world, stable and moving, with your vajra mind.
I bow to you, endowed with the body of inconceivable dharma.

Refined subtle essence purified by fire,
A body where infinite light-forms converge as one.
You are teacher, the taught, and the audience.
I bow to you, body of enjoyment, in all of the ways.

Like the moon reflected in clear water,
Endowed with the splendor of compassion, emanating at random
Again and again in the realms of six beings,
Ever appearing, I bow to you with respect.

Teaching the great perfection of clear light, the peak of nine vehicles,
Jeweled parasol covering the range of snowy mountains,
Its handle, the essence of teaching and practice;
Pray, raise it for the glory of myriad fortunate ones.

Treasury of the secret heart essence of Lotus Vajra,
Gateway to the treasure of one hundred and seven indestructible precepts
Opened by the magic of illusory wisdom,
The fame of its wonder blazes ever higher in the world.

With one hundred gateways of diverse and skillful emanations,
Linking the tradition of the majestic Padma
Even to the end of this time of five hundred degenerations,
Crown ornament of a hundred adepts, I bow to Ter-dak ling-pa.[15]

. ༡༦ .

བཅོམ་ལྡན་འདས་མ་གསུང་གི་དབང་ཕྱུག་ལ་ཕྱག་འཚལ་ལོ། །

དབྱངས་ཅན་རིག་པ་མ་སྨད་འདི། །
ངེས་པར་ངག་རྣམས་གསལ་བྱེད་དེ། །
འཇིག་རྟེན་གསལ་བྱེད་ངག་གིས་ནི། །
ཁྱེད་ཅག་མཁྱེན་པ་མཛེས་གྱུར་ཅིག།

བཀྲ་ཤིས་གཞུང་འདིར་སྨོན་བྱུང་བ། །
བརྟན་དང་བསམ་པ་བཟང་ལྡན་པའི། །
མཆོག་གི་ལམ་ལ་རྗེས་ཞུགས་པའི། །
ཁྱུ་མཆོག་ལེགས་འཆང་སྭ་རའོ། །

དེ་ཡི་རྣམ་དཔྱོད་རབ་ཡངས་ཉིད། །
རྒྱུ་སྐར་བྲལ་བའི་མཁའ་ཡིན་ཏེ། །
ཉིན་བྱེད་འོད་ལྡན་འཛོག་ལྡན་མའི། །
བགྲོད་པའི་གནས་ནི་འདི་མ་ཡིན། །

. ༡༧ .

སྙིང་རྗེའི་བདག་ཉིད་ཕྱག་ན་པདྨོ་དང་། །
དབྱེར་མེད་ཆོས་ཀྱི་རྗེ་གཅིག་ཞབས་དཀར་བ། །
གང་གི་རྣམ་ཐར་ཚངས་པའི་ཛ་བོ་ཆེ། །
གྲངས་མེད་འགྲོ་འདིའི་བསོད་ནམས་ཞིང་གིས་བཀུགས། །

མཐོན་པོའི་ས་ལ་གནས་ནས་རིགས་པའི་གཞུང་། །
མ་ལུས་ཁྱེད་ཐུགས་དྭངས་པའི་མེ་ལོང་དུ། །
འགོག་མེད་འཆར་བའི་ངོ་མཚར་རྨད་བྱུང་ཚུལ། །
རིང་མོ་ཞིག་ན་ཡང་དག་རྫོགས་ལགས་ཀྱང་། །

སྡུག་བསྔལ་བརྒྱ་ཡིས་ཉེན་པའི་སྐྱེ་དགུ་ཡི། །
བློ་དང་འཚམས་པར་གོ་སླའི་ངག་ཚིག་གིས། །

. 16 .

Homage to the Lady of Speech.

This supreme intellect Sarasvatī
Illuminator of speech;
May you adorn my throat
With words to clarify the world.

An ocean bears her, leading followers
To the supreme path
Of sacred diligence and reflection
Upon the auspicious purāṇas.

The expanse of her intelligence
Is a sky free of stars;
This is no place for a ladder
Leading to the shining sun.[16]

. 17 .

Shab-kar-wa, sole lord of the dharma
Inseparable from Padmapāṇi, embodiment of compassion,
Whose life story is Brahmā's drum,
Summoning countless migrators with the richness of his merits.

Abiding at a lofty stage, all treatises on logic
Were perfected long ago in wondrous ways,
Appearing without obstruction
In the mirror of your clear mind.

Yet with words easy to understand, suited to the minds
Of beings beset by a hundred sufferings,

ཟབ་མོའི་ཆོས་ཀྱང་བདེ་བླག་འདོམས་མཛད་པ། །
སྙིགས་དུས་བཤེས་གཉེན་ཁྲིད་ན་ཁྲིད་ཉིད་ཙམ། །

རང་བཞིན་དག་པའི་བློ་གྲོས་ཤེལ་གྱི་ཁམས། །
གཞུང་ལུགས་ཆེན་བརྒྱའི་མདངས་ཀྱིས་ཁ་བསྒྱུར་བའི། །
ལྷན་ཅིག་སྐྱེས་པའི་ཡོན་ཏན་ལྷ་ཡི་ཁྱིམ། །
རྟག་ཏུ་སྐྱོད་པའི་ཆོས་ཀྱི་བཤེས་གཉེན་ཁྱོད། །

. ༡༥ .

བྱམས་བརྩེའི་དཀྱིལ་འཁོར་རྣམ་རྫོགས་པ། །
བསྟན་འཛིན་བདེ་འབྱུང་གཙུག་གི་རྒྱན། །
འཕྲིན་ལས་སྣང་བས་གསེར་ལྡན་ཁྱོན། །
ཀུན་ཁྱབ་རྒྱལ་བ་རྒྱ་མཚོའི་མགོན། །

. ༡༦ .

ལྷོ་ཕྱོགས་འཛམ་གླིང་མ་ག་དྷར། །
སྟོང་གཉིས་དགུ་བརྒྱ་ལྔ་སྔོན་ལོ། །
གཞོན་ནུ་དོན་ཀུན་གྲུབ་པ་འཁྲུངས། །
ཐེག་ཆེན་ཆོས་ལུགས་ན་ལེན་ཏ། །
ཀླུ་སྒྲུབ་ཤིང་མོ་བྱ་ལོ་བར། །
ཉིས་སྟོང་བཞི་བརྒྱ་ཉེར་ལྔ་སོང་། །
བར་ལ་པཏ་ལི་པུ་ཏྲར་ཡུལ། །
ཆོས་རྒྱལ་མྱ་ངན་མེད་ཅེས་བྱུང་། །

He who teaches even the most profound doctrines with ease
Among virtuous friends of the degenerate age is but you.

The crystal realm of your pure intellect is
A divine abode of spontaneously created qualities
Shimmering with reflections of texts of a hundred colors.
You are the dharma friend, ever active.[17]

. 18 .

Your sphere of kindness is perfect,
Upholder of the teaching, source of joy, crown ornament.
The light of your deeds shines upon the golden realm.
Lord of the all-pervading ocean of victors.[18]

. 19 .

In Magadha in the southern continent Jambudvīpa
Two thousand nine hundred and five years ago
Prince Siddhārtha was born.
In the Year of the Female Wood Bird,
Two thousand four hundred and five years ago,
Nāgārjuna came to Nālandā for the Mahāyāna school.
In between, in the land of Pāṭaliputra
The dharma king named Aśoka appeared.[19]

. ༢༠ .

ཉ་གང་ཟླ་བ་ཤར་བར་སུ་ཞིག་སྐྱད། །
ཟམ་གཙང་སྲས་ཀྱི་ཞབས་ལ་སུ་མི་འདུད། །
འབྲུག་སྒྲ་སྒྲོག་པས་རྨ་བྱ་ཅིས་མི་དགའ། །
དམ་ཆོས་བདུད་རྩིས་བདག་ཡིད་ཅིས་མི་འཚེངས། །

. ༢༡ .

ལྷེམ་ལྷེམ་གཡོ་བའི་པདྨ་ལ། །
ཡང་ཡང་འཁོར་བའི་བུང་བ་བཞིན། །
བརྗེད་བརྗེད་ཡངས་པའི་གཏྟོ་ལས། །
ཡང་ཡང་གྲུས་པས་བསྐྱོད་པར་བྱེད། །

. ༢༢ .

མཐོང་ན་འཇིགས་པའི་བདེན་པ་གཅེར་བུ་ལ། །
རང་མགོ་བསྐོར་བའི་གོས་ཀྱིས་མི་གཡོགས་པ། །
འདི་ནི་མཁས་པའི་དམ་ཚིག་དང་པོ་སྟེ། །
སྒྲིག་ལ་བབས་ཀྱང་འབད་པས་བསྲུང་བར་འཚལ། །

. ༢༣ .

ཆག་གྲུམ་ཆ་ཤས་ཆེད་དུ་བསལ་བ་ལ། །
ཕྱོགས་སྔའི་འབེན་དུ་བཀོད་དེ་མཚོན་བསྣུན་པའི། །
རང་སྡེ་མཁས་པའི་དགྲ་ལྷའི་དཔུང་བསྐྱོད་འདིས། །
གཞན་སྡེའི་དཔའ་བོ་ད་དུང་བསད་པ་མིན། །

. 20 .

Who would reproach the shining of the full moon?
Who would not bow at the feet of Śuddhodana's son?
What peacock does not rejoice at the thunderclap?
Why would my mind be unsatisfied with the ambrosia of true dharma?[20]

. 21 .

Like a bee circling again and again
Around a gently swaying lotus,
In the vast and splendid temple,
I am moved by devotion again and again.[21]

. 22 .

The naked truth, terrifying to behold,
Is not to be covered with robes of self-deception.
This is the first vow of the scholar.
Please keep it though it costs you your life.[22]

. 23 .

In order to refute their opponents over some fragments,
Our learned ones set up the target and pierce it with a weapon.
Yet by singing songs of praise to the gods of war,
The hero of the other side is still not slain.

ཇི་ལྟར་དངོས་པོའི་གཤིས་ལ་ཉེ་གྱུར་པ། །
དེ་ལྟར་མཁས་པའི་ཚིག་ནི་ལྐུགས་འགྱུར་བས། །
རང་བཞིན་ཉིད་ཀྱིས་ཕྲ་བའི་ཆོས་རྣམས་ཀུན། །
སླ་བསམ་བརྗོད་པའི་ཡུལ་ལས་འདས་པར་བཤད། །

. ༢༨ .

གསུངས་པ་རེ་ལ་དགོངས་པ་མཐའ་ཡས་ཤིང༌། །
བསམ་པ་རེ་ལ་འཆར་སྒོ་གྲངས་མེད་ཕྱིར། །
གོ་བར་དཀའ་བའི་རྡོ་རྗེའི་ཚིག་རྣམས་ལ། །
གོ་ཆོད་མ་ལུས་དོན་དུ་འགྲེལ་བར་བྱ། །

. ༢༩ .

ཇི་ལྟར་དངོས་པོའི་གཤིས་ལ་ཉེ་གྱུར་པ། །
དེ་ལྟར་མཁས་པའི་ཚིག་ནི་ལྐུག་འགྱུར་བས། །
རང་བཞིན་ཉིད་ཀྱིས་ཕྲ་བའི་ཆོས་རྣམས་ཀུན། །
སླ་བསམ་བརྗོད་པའི་ཡུལ་ལས་འདས་པར་བཤད། །

རྣམ་ཀུན་སྟོང་པའི་ཆོས་ལ་ཐུགས་བཞག་སྟེ། །
དེ་བཞིན་གཤེགས་པས་ཕྱག་གིས་མ་ཁིགས་པའི། །
སྣང་བའི་སྨིག་སྒྱུ་འཁྲིགས་པའི་འཁོར་བ་འདིར། །
ཡོད་མེད་ཁས་ལེན་བློ་ཡིས་ཐོང་བ་སུ། །

. ༢༦ .

བདུད་ཀྱི་མཚོན་ཆ་རྒྱུ་བ་མོ་དག་ལ་འཇམ་མཉེན་མེ་ཏོག་ལན་དུ་སྦྱིན། །
ལྷས་བྱིན་ཁྲོས་པའི་སྒྲོགས་རྡོ་འཕངས་ཆེ་མི་སླུའི་བརྟུལ་ཞུགས་དང་དུ་བླངས། །

As they draw near to the nature of things
The words of the learned become mute.
All phenomena, subtle by their very nature,
Are said to be beyond expression in words or thoughts.[23]

. 24 .

For each statement [of the Buddha] there are limitless intentions,
For each motivation there are countless ideas.
Explain the adamantine words, so difficult to fathom
To mean anything you might imagine.[24]

. 25 .

As they draw near to the nature of things
The words of the learned become mute.
All phenomena, subtle by their very nature,
Are said to be beyond expression in words or thoughts.

The mind is placed in the nature of the emptiness of all things.
In this saṃsāra, thick with the mirages of appearance
That even the Tathāgata's hand cannot stop,
Who can let go of belief in existence and nonexistence?[25]

. 26 .

To the sharp weapons of the demons, you offered delicate flowers in return.
When the enraged Devadatta pushed down a boulder, you practiced
silence.

རང་གི་དགྲ་ལ་སྡང་མིག་ཙམ་ཡང་བལྟ་བར་མི་ནུས་ཤཱཀྱའི་སྲས། །
འཇིགས་རྟེན་འཁོར་བའི་དགྲ་ཆེན་སྐྱོབས་པའི་གྲོགས་སུ་ཤེས་ལྡན་སུ་ཡིས་བཀུར། །

. ༢༧ .

ཡིད་ཀྱིས་མེད་པར་ཐག་ཆོད་ཅིང་། །
མིག་གིས་ཡོད་པར་མཐོང་བའི་ཚེ། །
ཞྭ་སེར་མཁན་པོས་མ་བསླབ་ཀྱང་། །
སྒྱུ་མའི་བློ་ལས་གཞན་ཅི་འབྱུང་། །

. ༢༨ .

ཡོད་མེད་བློ་ཡིས་བཞག་པའི་ཤེས་བྱ་དང་། །
བདེན་རྫུན་ཡུལ་ལ་ལྟོས་པའི་ཚད་མ་གཉིས། །
གཅིག་གི་རྫུན་ཁུངས་གཅིག་ལ་གཏད་མཐོང་ནས། །
ཐ་སྙད་ཚད་གྲུབ་འཇོག་ལ་བློ་མ་བདེ། །

མ་བརྟག་མ་དཔྱད་འཇིག་རྟེན་རྣམ་གཞག་དང་། །
བརྟགས་ཤིང་དཔྱད་པའི་གྲུབ་མཐའི་གཞུང་ལུགས་གཉིས། །
གཅིག་གི་རྩ་བ་གཅིག་ལ་ཐུག་མཐོང་ནས། །
ཐ་སྙད་ཚད་གྲུབ་འཇོག་ལ་བློ་མ་བདེ། །

བློ་ལ་སྣང་བ་ཙམ་གྱི་སྒྱུ་མ་དང་། །
དོན་ལ་ཡིན་པར་ངེས་པའི་གཤིས་ལུགས་གཉིས། །
གཅིག་ཤེས་བདེན་ན་གཅིག་ཤེས་རྫུན་མཐོང་ནས། །
ཐ་སྙད་ཚད་གྲུབ་འཇོག་ལ་བློ་མ་བདེ། །

རང་སྐྱོན་རི་བོ་འགེབ་པའི་སྡེ་གྲོལ་དང་། །
གཞན་སྐྱོན་ཁབ་ཀྱིས་འཚོལ་བའི་ཕྱི་གྲོལ་གཉིས། །
གཅིག་ལས་གཅིག་རྒྱལ་རེས་སུ་ཕྱེད་མཐོང་ནས། །
ཐ་སྙད་ཚད་གྲུབ་འཇོག་ལ་བློ་མ་བདེ། །

Son of the Śākyas, incapable of casting even an angry glance at your enemy,
What intelligent person would honor you as a friend for protection from
the great enemy, fearful saṃsāra?[26]

. 27 .

When one decides that it does not exist with one's mind
And sees that it exists with one's eyes,
Even without being taught by the yellow-hat abbot,
What can arise but awareness of illusion?[27]

. 28 .

Objects of knowledge posited by the mind as existent and nonexistent;
Valid forms of knowledge dependent on objects true and false.
Having seen that the source of falsity in one is entrusted to the other,
I am uncomfortable about positing the validity of convention.

The presentation of the unexamined, unanalyzed world;
The systems of tenets that examine and analyze.
Having seen that the foundation of one rests on the other,
I am uncomfortable about positing the validity of convention.

Illusions that are mere appearances to the mind;
The mode of being determined to be real.
Having seen that if one is true, the other is false,
I am uncomfortable about positing the validity of convention.

The first speaker hides the mountain of his own faults;
His opponent searches for the other's faults with a needle.
Having seen them take turns defeating each other,
I am uncomfortable about positing the validity of convention.

ཡོད་མཐའ་འགོག་པའི་སྣང་ཙམ་མ་དམིགས་དང་། །
མེད་མཐའ་སྤོང་བའི་མི་སྣང་མ་དམིགས་གཉིས། །
གཅིག་གི་རྣམ་གཞག་གཅིག་གིས་བཞིག་མཐོང་ནས། །
ཐ་སྙད་ཚད་གྲུབ་འཇོག་ལ་བློ་མ་བདེ། །

གྲོགས་པོ་མཚན་མར་ཞེན་པའི་བདེན་འཛིན་དང་། །
གྲོགས་ཀྱིས་ཕན་པར་རྟོགས་པའི་ཚད་མ་གཉིས། །
སྲིད་པ་སྐྱེད་ལ་ཁྱད་པར་མི་འདུག་པས། །
ཐ་སྙད་ཚད་གྲུབ་འཇོག་ལ་བློ་མ་བདེ། །

དགྲ་བོ་བདེན་པར་ཞེན་པའི་དངོས་འཛིན་དང་། །
དགྲ་ཡིས་གནོད་པར་ངེས་པའི་ཚད་མ་གཉིས། །
ཞེ་སྡང་སྐྱེད་ལ་ཁྱད་པར་མ་མཐོང་ནས། །
ཐ་སྙད་ཚད་གྲུབ་འཇོག་ལ་བློ་མ་བདེ། །

རྗེས་དཔག་ཚད་མ་མངོན་སུམ་བློ་ལས་སྐྱེས། །
མངོན་སུམ་བདེན་རྫུན་རྗེས་སུ་དཔག་པས་དཔྱད། །
ཕ་ཡི་དཔང་པོ་བུ་ཡིས་བྱས་པ་འདྲེས། །
ཐ་སྙད་ཚད་གྲུབ་འཇོག་ལ་བློ་མ་བདེ། །

རིགས་པས་དཔྱད་པ་ཤིང་རྟའི་སྲོལ་ལ་བརྟེན། །
ཤིང་རྟ་ཆེན་པོ་རིགས་པའི་སྟོབས་ཀྱིས་སྒྲུབ། །
རང་ཐག་ཆོད་ན་སུ་ཡི་རྗེས་སུ་འབྲང་། །
རང་ཐག་མ་ཆོད་སུ་ལ་ཡིད་རྟོན་བྱེད། །

ཡང་དག་རིགས་པ་ངེས་དོན་ལུང་ལས་རྙེད། །
དྲང་ངེས་ཁྱད་པར་དྲི་མེད་རིགས་པས་འབྱེད། །
རིགས་པས་ཤེས་ན་ངེས་དོན་ཅི་ལ་འཚོལ། །
རིགས་པས་མ་ཤེས་ངེས་དོན་ག་ལ་རྙེད། །

The nonobservation of what is suitable to appear negates the extreme of existence;
The nonobservation of what does not appear abandons the extreme of nonexistence.
Having seen that the presentation of one is destroyed by the other,
I am uncomfortable about positing the validity of convention.

Because there is no difference in the attachment produced
By the conception of true existence that holds a friend to be real and
By the valid knowledge which understands that friends are helpful,
I am uncomfortable about positing the validity of convention.

Having seen no difference in the hatred produced
By the conception of real existence that holds an enemy to be true and
By the valid knowledge which determines that enemies are harmful,
I am uncomfortable about positing the validity of convention.

Inferential valid knowledge is produced from direct perception;
Inference analyzes whether direct perception is true or false.
Because the child is serving as the father's witness,
I am uncomfortable about positing the validity of convention.

Analysis by reasoning depends on the founders' systems;
The founders are established by the power of reasoning.
If I can decide on my own, whom should I follow?
If I cannot decide, on whom can I rely?

Correct reasoning is found in definitive scriptures;
The provisional and definitive are distinguished by stainless reasoning.
If one understands with reasoning, why search for definitive meaning?
If one does not understand with reasoning, how does one find definitive meaning?

བྱམས་མགོན་ཁྲི་མོར་མཐོང་བའི་ངང་ཚུལ་འདིས། །
མ་བརྟགས་ལྷན་སྐྱེས་བློ་ལ་ཡིད་མ་ཆེས། །
དབུ་སེམས་མཁན་པོའི་ལྷ་གྲུབ་འགལ་ལུགས་འདིས། །
དཔྱོད་ལྡན་མཁས་པའི་བློ་ལ་ཡིད་མ་ཆེས། །

ཕལ་པ་དྲང་པོའི་རྗེས་སུ་འབྲང་འབྲང་ནས། །
རྒྱུད་པའི་རྩ་བ་ལྷན་སྐྱེས་བདེན་འཛིན་ཉིད། །
མཁས་པ་དྲང་པོའི་རྗེས་སུ་འབྲང་འབྲང་ནས། །
དེ་ལས་སྤྲུག་པའི་ཀུན་བརྟགས་བདེན་འཛིན་ཉིད། །

ཡོད་མེད་ཡིན་མིན་བདེན་རྫུན་ལ་སོགས་པའི། །
རྟོད་པའི་ཁུར་སྒྲ་སྒྲོག་པའི་འཇིག་རྟེན་འདིར། །
རྟག་ཏུ་གང་མཐོང་ཤེས་བྱ་ཡིན་པར་སྣང་། །
རྒྱུན་དུ་གང་གོམས་ཚད་མ་ཡིན་པར་སྣང་། །

མི་མང་གང་ལ་དགའ་དེ་བདེན་པ་དང་། །
ཁ་མང་གང་ལ་མཐུན་དེ་གྲུབ་མཐར་སྣང་། །
མི་རེའི་ཁོང་ན་མི་མཐུན་ཚད་མ་རེ། །
དེ་ཡི་རྒྱབ་སྐྱོར་རྡོ་རྗེའི་བཀའ་ལུང་རེ། །

ལ་རེའི་རྒྱབ་ན་མི་མཐུན་ཆོས་ལུགས་རེ། །
དེ་ཡི་རྗེས་འབྲང་མཁས་བླུན་སྟོང་ཕྲག་རེ། །
འདི་ཉིད་བདེན་ལ་འདི་ཡིས་མི་བསླུ་ཞེས། །
རང་གི་བདེན་ཁ་རང་ལ་སྦྱིན་པ་འདི། །
རིགས་མཐུན་སྐྱེ་བོའི་ཚོགས་རྣམས་ཉམས་རེ་དགའ། །
མི་མཐུན་ཚོགས་ལ་སྨྲས་ན་ཞེ་རེ་ཁྲེལ། །

མི་མཐུན་རིགས་དྲུག་འགྲོ་བའི་རྒྱལ་ཁབ་འདིར། །
བཅུ་ཡིས་འདོད་པ་བརྒྱ་ཡིས་མི་འདོད་ཅིང་། །
མི་ཡིས་མཐོང་བ་ལྷ་ཡིས་མི་མཐོང་བས། །
བདེན་རྫུན་ཚད་མའི་ཁྲིམས་ཐག་སུ་ཡིས་ཆོད། །

Because of this way in which Maitreyanātha was seen as a female dog,
I do not believe in the unanalyzed, innate mind.
Because of this way in which the views of Madhyamaka and Cittamātra
abbots contradict each other,
I do not believe in the minds of analytical scholars.

Vulgar people, having repeatedly followed what is right,
Find the innate conception of true existence; it is the root of all downfall.
Scholars, having repeatedly followed what is right,
Find the artificial conception of true existence; it is worse than that.

In this world where there resounds the noise of debate
About existence and nonexistence, is and is not, true and false,
Whatever is constantly seen appears as an object of knowledge.
Whatever one has always known appears to be valid.

Whatever most people like appears as the truth;
Whatever most mouths agree on appears as dogma.
Inside each person is a different valid form of knowledge,
With an adamantine scripture to support it.

Beyond each mountain pass is a different religious sect
With thousands of scholars and fools who follow, saying,
"Just this is true; this will not deceive you."
This self-authorization of one's own truth
Delights a group of like-minded beings.
When told to a group that does not agree, they are scornful.

Here in the capital of six types of beings who cannot agree,
What is asserted by ten is not asserted by a hundred;
What is seen by humans is not seen by gods.
Who makes the laws that validate truth and falsity?

ཤེས་རབ་སྦྱངས་པས་མི་ཆེ་ཟད་བྱས་པའི། །
གྲུབ་མཐའ་མཁན་པོའི་བློ་ཡང་འཁྲུལ་གྱུར་ན། །
འཇིག་རྟེན་བླུན་པོའི་རྫུན་གྱི་སྣང་བ་ལ། །
ཐ་སྙད་ཚད་མར་ཡིད་རྟོན་བྱེད་པ་འཁྲུལ། །

མཁོ་ཚད་བཟང་ཚད་སེམས་ཀྱི་འཆར་སྒོ་ཀུན། །
གུད་དུ་ཕྱེ་ནས་ཚད་མར་འདོད་པ་དེས། །
སྒྱུ་མའི་གྲོང་ཁྱེར་ཞིག་པའི་ཐང་སྟོང་དུ། །
མིག་འཕྲུལ་ནོར་བུའི་ཕུང་པོ་སླར་ཡང་རྙེད། །

བཞིན་རས་ཅུང་ཟད་འགྱུར་བས་འགྱུར་བྱེད་ཅིང་། །
མེ་ལོང་ཅུང་ཟད་འགྱུར་ཡང་འགྱུར་བྱེད་པའི། །
མི་བརྟན་འགྱུར་བའི་ཤེས་བྱའི་གཟུགས་བརྙན་འདི། །
ནམ་ཞིག་མཐའ་ལ་གཏན་དུ་ཡལ་བར་ངེས། །

དཔྱད་པ་འདི་ལ་ཐུག་པས་མེད་དམ་སྙམ། །
ལག་པ་ཁབ་ལ་འཕྲད་པས་ཡོད་དམ་སྙམ། །
སྤྱོང་བ་མངོན་སུམ་ལག་པས་ཡིན་ནམ་སྙམ། །
སྣང་བ་འཁྲུལ་པ་སྲིད་པས་མིན་ནམ་སྙམ། །

ཡོད་པའི་རྒྱ་བ་བཙལ་བས་མེད་དམ་སྙམ། །
མེད་པའི་རྒྱུ་མོ་མཐོང་བས་ཡོད་དམ་སྙམ། །
བདེན་པའི་ས་བོན་བཏབ་ན་རྫུན་པར་ཤེས། །
རྫུན་པའི་འབྲས་བུ་སྨྱོང་ཆེ་བདེན་པར་སྣང་། །

. ༢༧ .

རྣམ་སྨིན་ལུས་དྲུག་ལྡན་པའི་རིགས་དྲུག་ལ། །
སྣང་བ་རྣམ་དྲུག་འབྱུང་བ་སྨོས་ཅི་དགོས། །
དབང་པོ་དྲུག་ལྡན་མི་ཡི་ལུས་ལ་ཡང་། །
ཐུན་མོང་རྒྱ་བ་མེད་པའི་སྣང་བ་དྲུག།

If there can even be mistakes in the mind of a philosopher,
Who has consumed his human life training in wisdom,
Then it is mistaken to be confident that
False perceptions of the fools of the world are conventionally valid.

All the things that seem to the mind to be useful and good
Are separated out and asserted to be valid.
Therefore, in the ruins of a magical city in an empty plain,
One finds the illusion of a pile of jewels once again.

This reflection of objects of knowledge, inconstant and changing—
By changing the face slightly, it changes,
By changing the mirror slightly, it also changes—
Is certain to vanish completely in the end.

Because analysis comes to this, I wonder whether it does not exist.
Because the hand touches a needle, I wonder whether it exists.
Because experience is direct, I wonder whether it happened.
Because perception can be mistaken, I wonder whether it did not happen.

Because we seek the root of existence, I wonder whether it does not exist.
Because we see the peak of nonexistence, I wonder whether it exists.
When we plant the seed of truth, we know it to be false.
When we taste the fruit of the false, it seems to be true.[28]

. 29 .

What is there to say about six types of appearance arising
For the six types of beings with six fruitional bodies?
There are six appearances without a shared foundation
Even for the bodies of humans with six sense organs.[29]

ཡོད་མེད་གཉིས་ལས་འདས་པའི་ཡེ་ཤེས་ནི། །
ཀླུ་སྒྲུབ་ཡབ་སྲས་དགོངས་པ་ཟབ་མོའི་གནད། །
གངས་ཅན་གསར་རྙིང་དམ་པ་གོང་མ་ཡིས། །
བཞེད་སྲོལ་གཅིག་ཏུ་དྲིལ་བའི་ལེགས་བཤད་འདི། །

ཁོ་བོའི་བླ་མའི་ཐུགས་རྗེའི་དགོངས་གླིང་ནས། །
མཁྱེན་པའི་ཉི་མ་ཕྱོགས་སུ་འཆར་བའི་ཚེ། །
དམུས་ལོང་ལོག་རྟོག་སྙིང་ལ་གཟན་ན་ཡང་། །
མིག་ལྡན་བློ་ཡི་གེ་སར་འཛུམ་པར་གྱུར། །

ཕྱོགས་དུས་རྒྱལ་བ་ཡོངས་ཀྱི་དགོངས་པའི་བཅུད། །
ལུང་རིགས་མན་ངག་བསྡེབ་བཅད་བརྡར་བའི་དབྱིག།
ཆོས་དབྱིངས་བསམ་མི་ཁྱབ་པའི་ས་ལེ་སྦྲམ། །
བདག་གི་སྙིང་ལ་འཆར་བ་སྨོན་གྱི་ལམ། །

འོན་ཀྱང་འཇམ་མགོན་བླ་མའི་ཞལ་ཆབ་ཀུན། །
ཆོས་ཀྱི་འཁོར་ལོར་འཁྱིལ་བའི་ལེགས་བཤད་མཚོར། །
མ་རིག་འདམ་གྱིས་རྙོག་པའི་ཆ་མཆིས་ན། །
གཞུར་གནས་བློ་ལྡན་ཚོགས་ལ་སྙིང་ནས་བཤགས། །

འདིར་འབད་ལེགས་བཤད་ཉི་མའི་འོད་ཟེར་ནི། །
དྭན་དབང་བློ་ཡི་པདྨོར་འཆར་བའི་མོད། །
རང་བྱུང་ཡེ་ཤེས་སྦྲང་རྩིའི་ཟིལ་མངར་བཅུད། །
རྣམ་ཀུན་ཞི་བའི་ངོ་བོར་སྨིན་གྱུར་ཅིག།

ཚེ་རབས་ཀུན་ཏུ་བླ་མས་རྗེས་འཛིན་ཞིང་། །
ཆོས་ཉིད་ཟབ་མོ་སྤྲོས་པ་བྲལ་བའི་དབྱིངས། །
མ་ནོར་རང་གིས་ཚུལ་བཞིན་རྟོགས་ནས་ནི། །
རྣམ་དག་ལམ་གྱི་བགྲོད་པ་མཐར་ཕྱིན་ཤོག།

. 30 .

The wisdom beyond existence and nonexistence
Is the pith of the profound thought of Nāgārjuna, father and son.
This eloquent explanation distills into one the Snowy Land's traditions
Of the true forefathers of the new and ancient schools.

When from the expanse of my lama's compassionate mind
The sun of knowledge shone in all directions,
Though it pained the heart of one blinded by wrong views,
It caused the calyx of the mind of one with sight to smile.

The essence of the minds of all the victors in space and time,
The refined, cut, polished jewel of scripture, reasoning, instruction,
The gold of the inconceivable sphere of reality.
It is due to my past karma that I hold these in my heart.

Yet in all the water in the mouth of the lama Mañjunātha [Tsong kha pa],
The ocean of eloquence forming the wheel of the dharma,
If there is a part muddied by the swamp of my ignorance,
I confess it from my heart to the assembly of the impartial.

At the instant that the sun's rays of the eloquence I strove for here
Shine upon the lotus of the minds of scholars,
May sweet nectar, the honeydew of self-arisen wisdom,
Always ripen as the nature of peace.

May I be cared for in all my lives by the lama
And know without error and just as it is
The sphere of the profound nature of reality, free of elaboration,
And then proceed to the end of the path of purity.

རྣམ་དཀར་སྦྱོར་བ་སྟོང་གི་རླུང་ཤུགས་ཀྱིས། །
མེད་སྣང་འཁྲུལ་བའི་རྒྱལ་ཁབ་སྟོན་ཀའི་སྤྲིན། །
ཆོས་དབྱིངས་ནམ་མཁའི་གནས་སུ་རོ་མཉམ་སྟེ། །
སྐུ་གསུམ་རྒྱལ་བའི་ཉི་མ་འཆར་བར་ཤོག།

Through the strong wind of a thousand virtuous deeds,
May the autumn clouds over the capital of mistaken appearances of the nonexistent
Become of one taste in the sky of the sphere of reality,
And the sun of the triple-bodied victor shine forth.[30]

Laments of an Unknown Sage

ཀ་ཡེ་ཁོ་བོ་གཞན་དུ་སོང་རྗེས་སུ། །
ཁ་ནས་ཅི་བཤད་མེད་པའི་ཨ་ཁུ་འགས། །
ག་ཡང་གནས་ཚུང་འཁྲིན་ལས་རྒྱལ་པོ་ཡིས། །
ང་རྒྱལ་ཆེ་བས་སྤྱོད་དུ་མ་བཅུག་ཟེར། །
ཅ་དག་བྱེད་པའི་ཆོས་སྐྱོང་ཞིག་ཡོད་ན། །
ཆ་རྒྱུས་ཡོད་མེད་ས་ཆ་ཀུན་འགྲིམས་ནས། །
ཇ་ཚང་སྐམ་ལྕུག་སོགས་ཀྱི་ཚོང་བྱེད་པའི། །
ཉ་ཉོག་དེ་ཚོ་སྤྱོད་དུ་ཅི་ལ་བཅུག།
ཏ་ལའི་འདབ་བཞིན་ཤམ་ཐབས་རྫོག་ག་བརྒྱབ། །
ཐ་ཚད་ལག་ཆ་ལྕགས་གྱི་ཛ་ཤིང་བཟུང་། །
ད་ལྟ་དེ་ཚོ་བསྐྲད་ན་ཚོག་པ་ལ། །
ན་ཉིང་དོ་ཚོགས་ཧེ་མང་ཧེ་མང་རེད། །
པ་སངས་ལྷ་བུའི་དད་པ་མེད་པས་ན། །
ཕ་རོལ་གཞན་དུ་བསྐྲད་ཅེས་ཁ་ཅིག་སྨྲ། །
བ་ལང་མཛོ་མོ་བྱ་བྱིའུ་འབའ་འབུ་སོགས། །
མ་དག་སེམས་ཅན་དེ་ཚོ་ཅིས་མ་བསྐྲད། །
ཙ་ཏུར་མཆེ་ལྡན་གནས་ཚུང་རྒྱལ་པོ་ཡིས། །
ཚ་གྲང་དལ་དུབ་སྣ་ཚོགས་ཁྱད་བསད་ནས། །
ཛ་ཡའི་བསྟན་ལ་ཐོས་བསམ་བྱེད་མཁན་རྣམས། །
ཝ་མ་ཝུ་ལ་གཞན་དུ་སྐྲོད་དོན་མེད། །
ཞ་གོས་ལྷམ་སོགས་བཟང་བའི་བསྟན་བཤིག་དང་། །
ཟ་མ་ངན་ངོན་ཟ་བའི་བསྟན་བཤིག་གཉིས། །
འ་ཅག་རྣམས་ཀྱིས་བལྟས་ན་ཁྱད་ཆེ་ཡང་། །
ཡ་གིའི་རྒྱལ་པོས་གཟིགས་ན་ཁྱད་པར་མེད། །
ར་བསྐྱུས་བསེ་བསྐྱུས་ཤེས་པའི་ང་རྒྱལ་ཅན། །
ལ་ལྕུང་ཡུལ་གྲུ་གཞན་ལ་སྐྲོད་པ་ལས། །
ཤ་ཚང་དུད་ཚོང་བྱེད་པའི་ང་རྒྱལ་ཅན། །
ས་ཆ་གཞན་དུ་བསྐྲད་ན་ཅིས་མ་ལེགས། །
ཧ་ཧ་ཨེ་བདེན་རང་གིས་བསམ་བློ་ཐོངས། །

. 31 .

Hey! After I had gone away
Some nonsense-talking lamas
Said that Nechung, king of deeds,
Did not let me stay because I was too proud.
If he is a protector who purifies,
How could he permit those impure monks to stay,
Wandering all over, the known and unknown,
Selling tea, beer, and dried mutton?
Their lower robe hiked up, folded like palm leaves,
The worst carry weapons, knives, and clubs.
If they'd been expelled, it would be fine;
Between last year and this, there are more and more.
Because I lacked faith, pure as Venus,
Some say I was banished to far-off lands.
Why weren't impure beings banished
Like cows, female yaks, birds, and bugs?
There is no purpose in four-fanged king Nechung
To banish to who knows where
Those who study and ponder the Victor's teachings
Braving hardships of heat, cold, and fatigue.
Destroyers of the good dharma with fine hats, robes, and boots
And destroyers of the dharma who eat simple food;
When we look at them, there is great difference.
But when the king above [Nechung] looks at them, there is no difference.
Rather than banishing to distant mountain passes, valleys, and towns
Those who take pride in studying the books of Ra and Se,
Would it not be better to banish to another place
Those proudly selling meat, beer, and tobacco?
Ha ha. Consider whether this is true.

ཨ་ཁྲུ་དགེ་བཤེས་ཚོ་ལ་ཞིབ་ཏུ་དྲིས། །
དེ་སྐད་སྨྲ་བ་པོ་ཡང་ཐ་སྙད་པ། །
རིགས་པའི་སེང་གེ་སཾགྷ་བྷདྲོའི། །

༣༢

རྒྱ་ཆེན་དོན་གཉིས་གྲུབ་པའི་དགའ་སྟོན་ལ་རོལ་པའི། །
མ་འདྲིས་འགྲོ་བའི་རྒྱ་ལག་ཟས་གཙང་གི་སྲས་པོ། །
མཐའ་དང་ཟད་དུ་མེད་པའི་བྱིན་རླབས་ཀྱི་སྤྲང་ཆར། །
ཐུགས་རྗེའི་རྒྱུ་འཛིན་འཁྲིགས་པའི་གུར་ཁང་ནས་ཕོབ་ཅིག།

ཐང་ཆེན་ཕ་མཐའ་མེད་པའི་དུད་སྤྲིན་གྱི་སྤྲིས་མ། །
ཀང་གླིང་སྐད་བརྡ་བསྒྱུར་བའི་རྒྱུས་མེད་ཀྱི་གྲོགས་པོ། །
ཁ་དོག་སྔོ་ལྗང་ཤར་བའི་ཞིང་ཆེན་གྱི་རི་མིག།
སྣང་ཡུལ་གང་ལ་བལྟས་ཀྱང་སྐྱོ་ཉམས་ཤིག་འདུག་པ། །

ཉེ་འབྲེལ་འཁོར་གཡོག་འཛོམས་པ་ཚོང་འདུས་ཀྱི་མགྲོན་པོ། །
སྤོབས་འགྱུར་ཁེངས་དྲེགས་དར་བ་རྨི་ལམ་གྱི་ལོངས་སྤྱོད། །
སྐྱིད་སྡུག་སྤྲེལ་མའི་ཉམས་མྱོང་དབྱར་དགུན་གྱི་འགྱུར་ལྡོག།
བསམ་བཞིན་མ་བཅོས་ཤུགས་པའི་གླུ་དབྱངས་ཤིག་ཤོར་སོང་། །

མེད་ན་ལྟོགས་ཀྱི་དོགས་པས་བཟའ་བཏུང་གི་རྩོལ་སྒྲུབ། །
ཡོད་ན་ཟད་ཀྱི་དོགས་པས་ཁེ་ཚོང་གི་འདུ་འགོད། །
དོན་ཆུང་ལས་ལ་འབད་པའི་ཕྲེང་གོག་དེ་བགྲང་ནས། །
ཡུན་ཐུང་མི་ཚེ་ཕྲ་མོའི་ཕྲེང་ཐག་དེ་ཟད་སོང་། །

བྱས་ཀྱང་འཛད་དུ་མེད་པའི་འཇིག་རྟེན་གྱི་བྱ་གཞག།
བྱས་བྱས་ལས་ཀྱི་མཐའ་ལ་ཡིད་ཆད་ཀྱི་སྟོན་པ། །
བྱས་ནས་གྲུབ་པར་རློམས་པའི་བདེ་འབྱོར་ཀུན་བསགས་ཀྱང་། །
སྡུག་བསྔལ་ཕུང་པོ་འདི་ཡི་བཅུ་ཆ་ལས་མི་འདུག།

ཁྲམ་དང་གཡོ་སྒྱུའི་རྩེད་མོ་དགུ་སྒྲིག་ཏུ་བྱས་ཏེ། །
འབད་པ་བརྒྱ་ཡིས་སྒྲུབ་པའི་འཇིག་རྟེན་གྱི་འདུན་མས། །

Carefully ask the elder geshes too.
The speaker of these words is the sophist,
Saṃghadharma, lion of reasoning.[31]

. 32 .

Son of Śuddhodana, friend to transmigrators unfamiliar,
Delighting in the festival that fulfills two vast aims,
Send down the seasonal rains of blessing, without limit or end
From the pavilion of dense clouds filled with the water of compassion.

The froth of clouds of smoke on a great endless plain,
An unfamiliar friend plays a thighbone trumpet,
The pattern of a huge land where five colors shine;
Whatever I see, I am melancholy.

The relatives and servants we meet are but guests on market day.
The rise of power, wealth, and arrogance are pleasures in a dream.
Happiness alternates with sorrow, summer changes to winter.
Thinking of this, a song spontaneously came to me.

When we lack it, fearing hunger, we seek food and drink.
When we have it, fearing loss, we arrange our gathered profits.
Slowly counting the beads of an old rosary, striving at such petty affairs,
The thread of this short human lifespan comes to its end.

Worldly affairs, no matter what they are, never end.
At the end of doing deeds, there grows despair.
When all pleasures and wealth proudly gained are gathered,
They make up but one-tenth this pile of pain.

Matching the games of lies and deception
With worldly schemes, pursued with great pains,

ཡུན་རིང་སྒྲུགས་པའི་མཐའ་ལ་སྟོང་བསྒྲུས་སུ་བྱས་པས། །
ལོ་གསུམ་སྡུག་ལས་བྱས་པའི་ཨ་ཐང་ནི་ཆད་སོང་། །

འབྱོར་ཆེ་ཉེ་བའི་དྭང་ན་ཁྱུད་ཁྱད་དུ་འགྲོ་ཞིང་། །
རྒྱུད་ཆེ་རིང་བའི་ས་ནས་མཛུབ་ཀེར་གྱིས་འཕྱ་བ། །
དྲིན་བྱས་དྲིན་དུ་མི་གོ་གྲོགས་ངན་གྱི་གཤིས་ལ། །
བསམ་ཞིང་དུ་མ་དགོད་ཀྱི་སྣང་བ་ཞིག་ཤར་སོང་། །

ཤེས་བརྩོན་ཐོས་པ་ཅན་གྱི་ཉམ་ཆུང་གི་ཁ་སྐབས། །
བླུན་པོ་ནོར་རྒྱལ་ཁྱུར་བའི་དབང་ཤེད་ཀྱིས་བཙོམ་སྐེ། །
ཆོས་མཐུན་བཀུར་སྟིའི་བཞུགས་གྲལ་གོ་ལོག་ཏུ་བསྡེབས་ནས། །
སེང་གེ་ཁྲི་ཡི་གཡོག་ཏུ་འཁྱུར་ཚུལ་འདི་སྐྱོ་བ། །

ཟིན་མེད་དབྱར་དགུན་དུས་བཞིའི་སོ་ཚིས་ལ་འབད་ནས། །
དོན་མེད་གཡེང་བས་མི་ཚེ་སྟོང་ཟད་དུ་ཕྱིན་ཀྱང་། །
ད་དུང་སྣང་མེད་གཡེང་བའི་འཕྱོར་ཉམས་དེ་ཆེ་བ། །
ལུས་ཀྲས་སེམས་མ་ཀྲས་པའི་སྣང་ཚུལ་འདི་སྐྱོ་བ། །

ཚོགས་དྲུག་སྣང་བ་ཡུལ་གྱི་མེ་ཏོག་གི་ཐང་དུ། །
གཏོལ་མེད་རིག་པའི་བུ་ཆུང་ཕར་ཕར་ལ་འཁྱམས་པས། །
དོན་མེད་གནས་ལ་སེམས་པའི་དྲན་འདུན་གྱི་ལམ་སྲོལ། །
ད་ལྟ་རྗེས་མེད་བོར་བའི་སྣང་ཚུལ་འདི་སྐྱོ་བ། །

རི་བོ་སྒང་དྲུག་ལྗོངས་ནས་རི་དྭགས་བཞིན་འཁྱམས་ཏེ། །
ཐག་རིང་རྒྱུས་མེད་མི་ཡི་རྒྱལ་ཁམས་སུ་སླེབས་ནས། །
མདོ་མེད་འཕྱོར་མོའི་ཕྱོགས་ལ་རང་སེམས་དེ་ཤོར་ནས། །
དྲིན་ཅན་ཕ་མ་བརྗེད་པའི་བུ་ཙུལ་ང་སྐྱོ་བ། །

མ་རིག་རྣམ་རྟོག་འདྲེ་མོའི་གར་སྐབས་ཀྱི་རྗེས་སུ། །
མི་བདེན་འཁྲུལ་པའི་ཆོས་འདི་ཡོམ་ཡོམ་དུ་གཡོས་པས། །
དེ་རིང་མཐོང་བའི་ཟང་ཟིང་སང་ཉིན་ནི་བརྗེད་དེ། །
གང་ལ་གཏད་སོ་མེད་པའི་ངང་ཚུལ་འདི་སྐྱོ་བ། །

བལྟས་ན་སྐྱིད་སྐྱིད་འདྲ་བའི་འཇིག་རྟེན་གྱི་ཕུན་ཚོགས། །
ཐོབ་ན་རང་རང་སྐབས་ཀྱི་སྡུག་བསྔལ་རེ་འདུག་པས། །

After waiting so long, it turned to nothing, just deceit.
Three years of miserable labor have worn me down.

When you are rich, they slink up close;
When you are poor, they scorn you from afar with pointing fingers.
The nature of bad friends who do not know kindness as kindness;
I think of this; tears and laughter rise up in me.

[The talents of a humble scholar, seeking only knowledge
Are crushed by the tyranny of a fool, bent by the weight of his wealth.
The proper order is upside down.
How sad, the lion made servant to the dog.]

Endlessly busy with the work of the seasons, summer and winter,
Human life is wasted in pointless distraction.
Still, I indulge in the flamboyance of careless distraction.
How sad, this sense of being old in body, not old in mind.

On a flowery plain in the land of the mind's six objects
A child of uncertain knowledge wandered afar.
The way I used to think about meaningful things
Is now lost without a trace. I see this and it makes me sad.

Wandering like a deer from the realm of six ranges
To arrive in a distant kingdom of unfamiliar humans,
There I lost my heart to a glamorous fickle woman.
A wretched son who has forgotten his kind parents, I am sad.

Following the dance steps of the demoness of ignorant thoughts,
These false confusing phenomena move to and fro.
Material things seen today are forgotten tomorrow.
Being in this aimless state is sad.

When looked at, the marvels of the world seem pleasing.
When attained, each has its own suffering.

འཕྲུལ་སྣང་བདེ་བའི་གནས་སྐབས་རྨི་ལམ་ཙམ་སོང་རྗེས། །
ཅིས་ཀྱང་རང་སེམས་སྐྱོ་བའི་རྐྱེན་སྣང་རེ་འདུག་གོ།

རེ་དོགས་འཚོག་འགྱུའི་རྣམ་རྟོག་སྡུག་བསྔལ་གྱི་སྦྲུར་རྩེ། །
ཤུགས་འབྱུང་དགའ་བདེའི་ཉམས་ཀྱིས་འོ་མ་དང་འདྲེས་པས། །
བཟའ་བཏུང་ལོངས་སྤྱོད་ཕྱི་ཡི་སྐྱིད་ཆས་ཙམ་འགྲིགས་ཀྱང་། །
བློ་བདེ་གུ་ཡངས་ནང་གི་སྐྱིད་ཉམས་དེ་མི་འདུག།

ཆེ་འདོད་རེ་བའི་གཞི་མ་མེ་ནང་དུ་བསྲེགས་ཤིང་། །
མི་འདོད་ཁྲལ་གྱི་བཙུན་གཟུགས་ཐལ་དོང་དུ་བསྐྱུར་ཏེ། །
གང་དྲན་སེམས་རྗེས་འབྲང་བ་སྨྱོན་པ་ཡི་སྤྱོད་པས། །
ལྷོངས་དང་ལྷོངས་སུ་རྒྱུ་བའི་གུ་ཡངས་ཤིག་བྱུང་ན། །

ཚུལ་གསུམ་རྟགས་ཀྱི་རྫོང་གོག་རྨིག་མེད་དུ་བཤིག་ཅིང་། །
མཐའ་བརྒྱད་དམ་བཅའི་མདུད་པ་རང་ས་རུ་ཆད་དེ། །
གང་ཤར་སྣང་བ་གཞི་མེད་རྩ་བྲལ་དུ་གོ་ནས། །
ཞེ་བློ་གཏིང་ནས་བདེ་བའི་དགའ་སྤྲོ་ཞིག་བྱུང་ན། །

སྟོང་པ་མཐའ་དབུས་མེད་པའི་འོད་གསལ་གྱི་དབྱིངས་སུ། །
འཛིན་མེད་སེམས་ཀྱི་ངོ་བོ་རོ་གཅིག་ཏུ་ཐིམ་སྟེ། །
རང་སྐྱོང་བརྗོད་དུ་མེད་པའི་ཟག་མེད་ཀྱི་བདེ་བ། །
ཉིན་དང་མཚན་དུ་སྤྱོད་པའི་སྐལ་བཟང་ཞིག་བྱུང་ན། །

སྣང་བ་མི་རྟག་ཨ་མའི་ཁྲི་འཛུམ་གྱི་དཀར་ནག།
རི་སྐྱིད་རི་སྡུག་རང་ཉམས་རྗེས་དྲན་གྱི་སྐྱོ་གླུ། །
རྒྱུས་མེད་ཕྱི་མའི་རི་ལྷོངས་ཛྙྒལའི་ཡུལ་དུ། །
མདོ་མེད་འཁྱམས་པོ་དགེ་འདུན་ཆོས་འཕེལ་གྱིས་བླངས་སོ། །

After moments of brief happiness become but a dream,
There is always something that makes me sad.

Curdles of suffering, misconceptions beneath our hopes and fears,
Mix with the milk of the experience of spontaneous delight.
Although the comforts of food, drink, and possessions are all arranged,
The experience of inner happiness, content and carefree, is missing.

The basis of my ambition for greatness is consumed in fire;
The unwanted tax of the monk's robe is left in ashes;
If only I had the utter freedom to wander from one land to another
With a madman's behavior, chasing whatever comes to mind.

The castle of the threefold reason is utterly destroyed;
The knotty claims of the eight extreme views are severed at their site.
If only I had the joy of the deepest awareness,
Knowing that whatever appears is without foundation, has no basis.

Into the sphere of clear light, empty, without edge or center,
The nature of the mind, grasping nothing, dissolves as one taste.
If only I had the good fortune to practice this day and night,
Knowing for myself unspoken untainted bliss.

A sad song recalling fleeting appearances, my mother's changing frowns and smiles,
And my own experiences, sometimes happy, sometimes painful,
Was sung by the gullible wanderer Gendun Chopel,
In the land of Bengal, unfamiliar realm beyond the mountain range.[32]

༣༣

སྲིད་པའི་འཁྲོར་པ་ལ་ཁའི་ན་བུན། །
འདུས་པའི་སྙིང་གྲོགས་ཚོང་དུས་མགྲོན་པོ། །
མ་ངེས་སྐྱིད་སྡུག་མདང་གི་རྨི་ལམ། །
བསམ་ཞིང་བསམ་ན་སྙིང་པོ་མི་འདུག།

རྒྱུས་མེད་གཤིན་རྗེའི་ཕོ་ཉས་ཁྲིད་ནས། །
ཕྱི་མའི་འཕྲང་རིང་འགྲིམ་པའི་གྲོགས་ལ། །
སྐྱབས་ཀྱི་དམ་པ་རྩ་གསུམ་ལྷ་ཡིས། །
ཐུགས་རྗེ་ཅན་གྱི་སྐྱེལ་མ་མཛོད་ཅིག།

སྐྱེས་ནས་འཆི་བ་འཁོར་བའི་ཆོས་ཉིད། །
བསྒྱུར་དུ་མེད་པ་སྒྱུ་མའི་རང་མདངས། །
མི་བཟློག་གཤིན་རྗེ་རྒྱལ་པོའི་བཀའ་ཡིག།
ཉམས་ཆུང་གྲོགས་ཀྱི་སྙིང་དུ་སླེབས་སོང་། །

སྔོན་སྨོན་ལས་ཀྱི་ཆར་ཟིམ་བབས་ཚེ། །
ཡོད་ཡོད་འདྲ་བའི་དགུང་གི་འཇའ་ཚོན། །
དུང་སེམས་ཉི་མས་གསལ་དུ་སོང་ཚེ། །
མི་མཐོང་ནམ་མཁའི་དབྱིངས་སུ་ཡལ་སོང་། །

ན་གཞོན་ལང་ཚོའི་མེ་ཏོག་རྒྱས་དུས། །
ཡིད་ཀྱི་ཆུ་བོ་གཅིག་ཏུ་འདྲེས་པའི། །
འདྲིས་འདྲིས་ཆུང་གྲོགས་སེམས་ཀྱིས་འཚོར་ཡ། །
ད་ལྟ་རིགས་དྲུག་གང་དུ་ཡོད་ན། །

སྐྱིད་ཤོད་ལྷ་སའི་གྲོག་ཆུ་ཕྲ་མོ། །
ཞག་གསུམ་འཛོམས་པ་འགྲོགས་པའི་ཐ་མ། །
མི་རིང་འཕྲད་པའི་ཁ་ཆད་བྱས་པ། །
རྨི་ལམ་དང་ནས་མཇལ་དུས་སླེབས་སོང་། །

ཀུན་གཞོན་བར་མའི་སྐྱེ་བོ་མཐའ་དག།
ངེས་མེད་འཆི་བའི་སྣང་ཚུལ་མཐོང་ཡང་། །

. 33 .

The wealth of the world is mist on the mountain pass.
My closest friends, but guests on market day.
Uncertain joys and sorrows are last night's dream.
I think and think; they have no essence.

Led by the unknown envoy of Yama,
My friend wanders the long and narrow path to the next life.
Sublime refuge, three divine foundations,
Please be his compassionate guide.

Being born then dying is the nature of saṃsāra.
Its manifestation, the illusion that nothing changes.
The royal decree of relentless Yama
Has befallen my helpless friend.

When the drizzle of past prayers and deeds is falling
The afternoon rainbow appears, seeming so real.
When the sun of yearning begins to shine
It vanishes in the realm of invisible sky.

Dear childhood friend, radiant half of my heart,
When the flower of youth blossomed,
The streams of our minds mixed.
Where in the six realms could you be now?

At the end of three days of bountiful friendship
In the narrow riverbed of Gyishö Lhasa
We promised to meet before too long.
The time has come to meet within a dream.

All beings, old, young, those in between,
See what unpredictable death looks like.

ཚང་སྐྱེས་གྲོགས་ཀྱིས་བོར་བའི་ཕྲོགས་ལ། །
ནང་གི་དུང་སེམས་ཆོད་ཐབས་མི་འདུག།

ཤི་རྗེས་འཁྱོད་པ་བླུན་པོའི་ངང་ཚུལ། །
ལུས་སེམས་ཀྱུད་པའི་རྒྱུ་ལས་མེད་ཀྱང་། །
ཡུན་རིང་འདྲིས་པའི་སེམས་ཀྱི་བག་ཆགས། །
གོམས་པའི་ཤུགས་འདི་བཟློག་ཐབས་མི་འདུག།

ལུས་ཟུང་ཟད་ལ་གེང་ཙམ་གཟུགས་བརྙན། །
གསོན་དུ་རེ་བའི་ཁོ་ཐག་ཆད་དེ། །
འཆི་བའི་མིག་གིས་ཅེ་རེ་བལྟ་བའི། །
གཏམ་དེ་བདེན་ན་སྙིང་ལ་གཟན་པ། །

མ་བརྟགས་སེམས་ཀྱི་འཆར་ཚུལ་ཞིག་ལ། །
ད་དུང་དྲུང་ན་ཡོད་ཡོད་འདྲ་བ། །
དྲན་པའི་གཞུ་མོ་ནང་དུ་བཀུག་ཚེ། །
སྙིང་ཁོང་སྟོང་པའི་རྒྱུ་ལས་མི་འདུག།

བརྩེ་ཞིང་འགྲོགས་པའི་ཕྱི་ཐག་བསམས་ཏེ། །
མཆོག་གསུམ་བསླུ་བ་མེད་པའི་ཞིང་དུ། །
དགེ་བའི་དངོས་པོ་ཅུང་ཟད་བསྔུབས་པ། །
ཕྱི་མའི་ཡུལ་དུ་གྲོགས་ལ་བསྔོངས་སོ། །

. ༣༨ .

ཀ་ཆུ་ཡན་ཆད་ནག་ཆུ་མན་ཆད་ནས། །
ཁ་ཅིག་མགོ་བའི་སྐྱེ་བོ་མང་ན་ཡང་། །
ག་ལེར་བསམ་ན་རང་རེ་ཐ་སྙད་པའི། །
ང་རྒྱལ་དེ་ནི་དོན་གྱི་ང་རྒྱལ་ཡིན། །

Yet there is no means to end the inner grief
Of those left behind by childhood friends.

To feel remorse at someone's death is foolish;
It only ruins the body and mind.
Yet I cannot overcome the accustomed,
This habit of mind so long familiar.

As your body lay dying, a skeleton's image appeared;
Hoping only to remain alive,
You stared with death's eyes,
If what they say is true, it devours my heart.

In the way things appear to the ordinary mind,
You are still with me; you seem so real.
When the bow of memory is bent,
It only causes an empty heart.

Pondering how love and friendship endure,
I dispatch to my friend in the land beyond
The few good things I've done
In the field of the infallible three jewels.[33]

. 34 .

Up to the Kachu and down to the Nagchu
There are many men whose rhetoric is lofty.
Yet, if I think about it carefully,
This pride of mine, a lover of words, is true pride.[34]

. ༣༨ .

དགའ་བར་མཐོང་ཆེ་དྲུང་དུ་འདུད་ཕྱེད་ཅིང་། །
སྡུག་པར་མཐོང་ཆེ་རྒྱང་ནས་ཡིབ་ཕྱེད་པ། །
ཕལ་པའི་སྐྱེ་བོ་ཀུན་གྱི་ཆོས་ཉིད་འདི། །
སྔ་མོའི་དུས་ནས་ཁོ་བོས་ཤེས་པ་ལགས། །

འཕྱོར་པར་མཐོང་ཆེ་དྲུང་དུ་འདུས་ཕྱེད་ཅིང་། །
རྒུད་པར་མཐོང་ཆེ་རྒྱང་ནས་ཡིབ་ཕྱེད་པ། །
ཕལ་པའི་སྐྱེ་བོ་ཀུན་གྱི་ཆོས་ཉིད་འདི། །
སྔ་མོའི་དུས་ནས་ཁོ་བོས་ཤེས་པ་ལགས། །

མི་བསྲུན་བརླང་པོར་སྤྱོད་པའི་སྐྱེ་བོ་ལ། །
མགོ་བོ་གཅོད་པའི་ཁྲིམས་ལུགས་མ་མཛད་ན། །
སྙིང་རྗེའི་ལམ་ནས་ཚུལ་དེ་ལྡོག་པ་ལ། །
དམྱལ་བའི་སྡུག་བསྔལ་བསྟན་ལས་ཐབས་གཞན་ཅི། །

མི་ཡི་རྗེ་བོ་མི་དཔོན་ཆེན་པོའི་དྲུང་། །
མི་ཡི་མཐའ་མ་དགེ་འདུན་ཆོས་འཕེལ་གྱིས། །
མི་འཐུང་མི་འཐུང་ཨ་རག་མི་འཐུང་ཞེས། །
མི་དམངས་ཚོགས་པའི་དབུས་སུ་དམ་བཅའ་འབུལ། །

. ༣༩ .

རིང་ནས་འདྲིས་པའི་རང་ཁྱིམ་དངོས་ཟིན་ཅིང་། །
ཚེ་རབས་སྔ་མའི་ལས་ཀྱི་འཕྲོ་རྙེད་དེ། །
དུས་ཀྱི་མཐར་ཡང་རྫོགས་པའི་སངས་རྒྱས་གསུང་། །
གསར་དུ་བསྒྱུར་བའི་དགའ་བ་གང་གིས་མཚོན། །

མི་ལོ་བརྒྱད་བརྒྱའི་ཡུན་ལ་རྒྱ་གར་དུ། །
མ་སླེབས་ཕྱི་དལ་ཅན་གྱི་ལོ་ཙཱ་བ། །
ལེགས་སྦྱར་བསྟན་བཅོས་དངོས་སུ་ཀློགས་པ་ཞིག།
ད་ལྟ་མགྡྷ་ན་མཆིས་སོ་སྐད། །

. 35 .

When they see you in happiness, they bow down before you.
When they see you in sadness, they turn away and hide.
This nature of all ordinary beings
I have known from long ago.

When they see you prospering, they gather before you.
When they see you in decline, they turn away and hide.
This nature of all ordinary beings
I have known from long ago.

For people whose behavior is untamed and coarse,
If a law is not made to behead them,
What other way is there to compassionately change their ways
Than to teach them the sufferings of hell?

In the presence of the officials of the lord of humans
The marginal human Gendun Chopel says,
"I won't drink, I won't drink, I won't drink liquor."
I offer this promise to the assembled common people.[35]

. 36 .

Recognizing my own home, familiar from so long ago
And finding the remnants of my deeds from former lives,
How can I show my joy in translating anew, at long last,
This scripture of the perfect Buddha?

They say that today there is in Magadha
After a gap of eight hundred years in India,
A late-coming translator [from Tibet]
Who actually reads the Sanskrit treatises.[36]

༣༧

སིངྒལ་ཡི་གནས་བརྟན་སྡེ་པ་དང་། །
གངས་རིའི་ཁྲོད་ཀྱི་ཡོད་པར་སྨྲ་བ་གཉིས། །
སྟོན་པ་གཅིག་གིས་བསྐྱངས་པའི་སློབ་མ་སྟེ། །
བཅོ་བརྒྱད་སྡེ་པ་ཉུབ་པའི་ལྷག་མ་ཉིད། །

ཕྱག་རྒྱ་བཞི་ལྡན་བདེ་བར་གཤེགས་པའི་བཀའ། །
རིམ་གྱིས་བརྒྱུད་པ་གནས་བརྟན་སྡེ་པའི་ལུང་། །
སུ་ཏིག་འཁྲི་ཤིང་དགའ་བའི་འཕྲེན་ཡིག་འདི། །
གངས་ཅན་རི་བོའི་ཁོངས་སུ་འཁྱོལ་བར་བྱས། །

༣༨

བཙུན་པའི་ཆ་ལུགས་རིང་ནས་ཡལ་གྱུར་ཅིང་། །
འདུལ་བའི་སྤྱོད་ལམ་ཤུལ་དུ་མ་ལུས་ཀྱང་། །
གནས་བརྟན་དགེ་སློང་ཚོགས་དང་མཇལ་བ་འདི། །
ཚེ་རབས་སྔ་མའི་ལས་ཀྱི་འབྲས་བུར་ངེས། །

༣༩

མཐོ་རིས་ཐར་པའི་དངོས་རྒྱུ་མི་ཕྱེད་ཅིང་། །
གསེར་དང་དངུལ་གྱི་འདུ་སྙོ་མི་ཡོང་བའི། །
བར་མ་དོ་རུ་གནས་པའི་གནད་འདི་དག།
ཀུན་གྱིས་བོར་ཀྱང་ཁོ་བོས་ཞིབ་ཏུ་དཔྱད། །

. 37 .

A Sthaviravādin of Singhala,
A Sarvāstivādin of the Snowy Range;
Disciples protected by the same Teacher,
Sole remnants of the vanished eighteen schools.

Sugata's word, endowed with four seals,
Sthaviravādin scripture, passed down by stages,
I made this epistle, a pleasing pearl-handled cane,
Arrive in the realm of snowy mountains.[37]

. 38 .

Although the dress of a monk has long disappeared
And the practice of monastic discipline has left no trace,
This meeting with the assembly of elder monks
Must be the fruit of a deed in a former life.[38]

. 39 .

Not acting as a real cause of heaven or liberation,
Not serving as a gateway for gathering gold and silver,
These points that abide in the in-between,
Cast aside by everyone, these I have analyzed in detail.[39]

. ༨༠ .

དུས་གསུམ་རྗེན་པར་གཟིགས་པའི་མངོན་ཤེས་དང་། །
ཟློམ་པའི་འོལ་ཚོད་སྨྲ་བའི་སྤོབས་པ་གཉིས། །
གང་ལ་མེད་པའི་ཉམ་ཆུང་ང་འདྲ་དག།
སྙིག་གྱུར་ཡུལ་ལ་དཔྱོད་ཚུལ་འདི་ཙམ་ཉིད། །

. ༨༡ .

ཡ་མཚན་བུ་རམ་སྦྱར་བའི་སྦྲང་གི་ཆང་། །
ཡང་ཡང་འཐུང་བས་མགོ་བོ་དཀྲུགས་པ་ལ། །
རྫུན་གྱི་ལན་ཚྭ་བྲལ་བའི་གཙང་མའི་ཆུ། །
ནན་གྱིས་སྦྱིན་པའི་ངལ་བ་ཕོ་བོས་བྱས། །

. ༨༢ .

ལྷོ་ལམ་བྱེ་མ་ཅན་གྱི་ཐང་དུ་ངལ་བའི་རྐང་འགྲོས་རབ་བགོད་ཅིང་། །
ངམ་ནག་རྒྱ་མཚོའི་འོབས་ཀྱིས་བསྐོར་བའི་ས་ཡི་སྨུ་ཁྱུད་མངོན་བརྒལ་ཏེ། །
གཅེས་ཤིང་འཕང་བའི་སྲོག་གི་ཉག་ཐག་རལ་གྲིའི་སོ་ལ་དྲངས་པ་ལས། །
དཀའ་བའི་ལོ་ཟླ་རིང་མོ་ཟད་ནས་ཅི་ཞིག་ལྷར་སྐྱེས་གཞུང་འདི་གྲུབ། །

ཆེན་པོའི་ལུང་དང་གསེར་གྱི་མཐུལ་བཅས། །
བསྐུལ་བའི་སྐྱེས་བུ་སུ་ཡང་མ་མཆིས་ཀྱི། །
རིགས་པའི་དབྱིག་མཛོད་འདོར་ལ་འཕང་བའི་བློས། །
རང་གིས་དཀའ་བ་འཁུར་དུ་བླངས་ཏེ་བྲིས། །

དབང་འབྱོར་ཁྲག་ལ་རྔམས་པའི་མི་འབར་བའི། །
དམར་སེར་ཕྲག་དོག་མིག་ལ་ཆེར་འཇིགས་ཀྱང་། །

. 40 .

The clairvoyance that nakedly sees the three times,
The confidence to express one's whims with pride;
For a meek person like me who lacks them both,
This alone is the way to analyze hidden things.[40]

. 41 .

By repeatedly drinking the fabled beer
Made from amazing molasses, the head becomes drunk.
I am weary of always giving away
Pure water, free of the salts of falsity.[41]

. 42 .

Walking with weary feet to the plains of the sandy south,
Traversing the boundary of a land surrounded by the pit of dark seas,
Pulling the thread of my life—precious and cherished—across a sword's
sharp blade,
Consuming long years and months of hardship, I have somehow finished
this book.

Although there is no one to beseech me
With mandates from on high or maṇḍalas of gold,
I have taken on the burden of hardship alone and written this,
Concerned that the treasury of knowledge will be lost.

Though terrified by the orange eye of envy
In the burning flame of those bloodthirsty for power,

གནོག་ཆུང་ཐོས་པ་བསགས་པའི་བག་ཆགས་ལ། །
གོམས་པའི་རང་སེམས་རིགས་པའི་གཏམ་ལ་ཆགས། །

ཐོས་བརྩོན་ཤེས་རབ་ཅན་གྱི་སྙིང་གི་སྒོར། །
ཅི་སྙེ་ཞུགས་ན་འབད་པའི་འབྲས་བུ་སྙེ། །
སྐུགས་པའི་འཇམ་དང་ཕྱུག་པོའི་ལེགས་སོ་ལ། །
རེ་བའི་རྨི་ལམ་བདག་ལ་ནམ་ཡང་མེད། །

ཟས་དང་སྒོམ་གྱི་མཁོ་བ་ཟད་པའི་སྡུག་གི་ཕུང་པོ་ཞིག་གྱུར་ཅིང་། །
རྙེད་དང་བཀུར་བསྟིའི་རེ་ཐག་ཆད་པའི་ཙུས་གོང་ཚོགས་རྣམས་འཐོར་བ་ན། །
དཀའ་བས་བསགས་པའི་མང་ཐོས་ཕུང་པོ་ཡི་གེའི་གཟུགས་སུ་གྱུར་པ་འདིས། །
མ་མཐོང་གྲོགས་པོ་རྣམས་ཀྱི་མདུན་དུ་རྒྱ་ཆེན་ཕན་པའི་ལམ་མཚོན་ཤོག།

. ༨༣ .

རིགས་མཐུན་མི་ཡི་འགྲོ་བའི་སེམས་ཀྱི་འོད། །
ཕན་ཚུན་འཕྲོ་བའི་རྒྱུན་ལམ་ཉག་གཅིག་དེ། །
ལུས་ངག་རྣམ་རིག་སྲད་བུ་ཟུང་འབྲེལ་བའི། །
ཐ་སྙད་གླིག་གི་སྐད་པ་འདིར་མཐོང་ནས། །
གཡར་པོའི་ཕ་ཡུལ་གངས་ཅན་བོད་ལྗོངས་སུ། །
རྒྱུན་རིང་གནས་པའི་མགྲོན་ལ་རྒྱུས་ཆེ་པའི། །
གནའ་བོའི་བརྡ་དང་ཕྱིས་ཀྱི་ཐ་སྙད་ཀུན། །
ཐོར་བུ་སྡེབ་ཏུ་བསྡུས་ཏེ་བྲི་བར་བྱ། །

. ༨༨ .

རྗེ་སྒྲུབ་པའི་དབང་ཕྱུག་དྲིལ་བུ་བའི། །
ཡུམ་རྡོ་རྗེ་བཙུན་མོ་མཇལ་བའི་གནས། །

Accustomed to the habit of gathering what I have learned,
My mind is attached to reasonable talk.

If it somehow enters the door of a wise person, intent on learning,
Then the fruit of my labor will have been achieved.
For the smiles of the stupid and the approval of the rich,
I have never yearned even in my dreams.

When this ink-stained body's need for food and drink is finished,
When this collection of bones—its thread of hope for gain and honor snapped—is scattered,
Then may the forms of these letters, a pile of much learning amassed through hardship,
Reveal the path of vast benefit in the presence of my unseen friends.[42]

. 43 .

Seeing this thread of the lightning of language
Connecting strings of body, speech, and knowledge,
The light from the minds of humans of like nature
Creates the sole stream radiating to each other.
With the great familiarity of a long-staying guest
In the snowy realm of Tibet, my borrowed homeland,
I will gather into one place and record
All the scattered ancient terms and latter-day expressions.[43]

. 44 .

Today the vagabond has arrived
At Bodhiviṣa in the eastern land

ཡུལ་ཤར་ཕྱོགས་བོ་ཏྲི་བི་ཊ་དེར། །
དུས་ད་ལྟ་འཁྲུམས་པོ་སླེབས་ནས་ཡོད། །

ཚེ་སྔོན་ལས་ཟེར་བ་ཀླུང་གི་རྟ། །
ལམ་གར་འདྲའི་གཏད་སོ་མེད་པ་ཞིག།
ང་བོད་ཕྲུག་བོད་དུ་སྐྱེས་པ་ཡི། །
ཚེ་དུམ་གཅིག་རྒྱ་གར་ཡུལ་དུ་ཟད། །

ལོ་བཅུ་གཉིས་ཨ་ལོང་འཁོར་གྱི་བར། །
སྐྱིད་ཆེ་བའི་ཕ་ཡུལ་མ་མཐོང་ཞིང་། །
སྒོས་དྲིན་ཆེན་གྱི་མ་རྒན་མ་མཇལ་པ། །
འདི་བསམ་ན་བྲལ་བའི་སྙིང་ཀླུང་ལངས། །

བྱང་གི་བྱང་ལམ་རིང་མོ་དང་། །
ལྷོ་ཡི་རྒྱ་མཚོ་ཆེན་པོ་གཉིས། །
མི་སྙིང་སྟོབས་ཅན་གྱི་བགྲོད་ལམ་དེ། །
ཡིད་ཨ་ཐང་ཆད་པའི་རྩ་བ་གཅིག།

དཔལ་མཉམ་མེད་སྣར་ཐང་ཆོས་སྡེ་ཙ། །
རྗེ་ཀུན་མཁྱེན་མཆོག་སྤྲུལ་དེ་དང་མཇལ། །
མི་དམན་མཐོང་གི་སྣང་ཤེས་མི་འཛིན་པར། །
ཐུགས་དགྱེས་པའི་བཀའ་མོལ་ལྷུགས་པར་བསྩལ། །

སྤྱོད་འཇུག་འགྲེལ་བ་ཀྲུ་མིག་མ།
དེ་བཞིན་ཡང་དགོན་མ་ལ་སོགས། །
ང་ཐ་སྙད་རྒན་པོའི་ལག་ཡོངས་དེ། །
སླེབ་ན་གྲྭ་ཚང་གི་དཀྱིལ་འཛོག་ཡིན། །

ས་རྒྱ་གར་ཐང་གི་ཚ་བ་དེ། །
སོང་པའི་མི་ཡིས་སྨྱོང་བ་ལས། །
ཐོས་པའི་མི་ཡིས་དྲན་པར་དཀའ། །
ཁྱེད་སྒོམ་ཀྱང་ཐུགས་ལ་མི་འཆར་ཙམ། །

ཀླུང་སིལ་མ་ལངས་ཀྱང་མེ་ལྕེ་འདྲ། །
ཆབ་སིལ་མོ་འཐུང་ཀྱང་ཛ་ཀྲོད་ཙམ། །

The place to encounter Vajravārāhī,
Consort of Ghantapa, lord of adepts.

The wind horse, the so-called deeds of former lives,
Has no direction on the road.
I, a child of Tibet, born in Tibet,
Have spent a portion of my life in the land of India.

Completing the whole cycle of twelve years
Without seeing my delightful homeland and
Most of all, not meeting my kind old mother;
When I think about this, I feel pangs of separation.

The long northern path
And the great ocean in the south,
These are roads for those endowed with courage,
The one route that leads to weariness.

At the monastery of the glorious and incomparable Narthang
I met the omniscient supreme incarnation.
Not regarding me as an inferior person,
He generously engaged in pleasing conversation.

The commentaries on the *Bodhicaryāvatāra*,
Of Chu-mig-pa, Yang-gon-pa, and so forth
Fell into my hands, I, a seasoned lover of words.
If they arrived, they would be the monastery's centerpiece.

The heat of the plain of India is hard to imagine,
For those who have only heard of it.
Unless they have gone there and felt it,
You may ponder it, but it does not appear to the mind.

Even when the breeze blows, it is like a tongue of flame
Even when you drink cool water, it is like black tea

ཡིན་ཀྱང་ལྟབ་ལེགས་ད་ལྟའི་བར། །
ངེད་ལ་ཚ་བའི་ནད་མ་ཐེབས། །

ཡུལ་རྒྱུས་མེད་མི་ཡི་རྒྱལ་ཁམས་ན། །
ང་གྲོགས་མེད་ཀྱི་མི་པོ་རི་དགས་འདྲ། །
ཕྱོགས་འདི་འདྲའི་ལམ་ལ་གཏད་སོ་མེད། །
ཡུལ་འདིར་བསྡོད་ཀྱི་ས་ལ་ངེས་བཟུང་མེད། །

ངས་ཚེ་སྟོད་གླེགས་བམ་གྱི་བམ་ཁ་སྟུད། །
ཚེ་སྨད་ཚིག་རྩུབ་ཀྱི་ཁུར་པོ་འཁུར། །
མི་ཚེ་སྡུག་ལ་བསྐྱལ་བ་འདི། །
ཐ་སྙད་ཀྱི་བསྟན་པ་ལ་ཨེ་ཕན་ལྟ། །

ཚིག་ཅོང་བོ་རྗེ་ཡི་ཟུར་ཁ་ཅན། །
སྐབས་འདི་ལ་སྨྲ་དོན་མི་འདུག་སྟེ། །
སྡུག་ཁོག་པ་གཡུལ་གྱི་གང་བ་དེ། །
གྲོགས་འདྲིས་པ་ཅན་ལ་ངང་གིས་ཤོར། །

གྲོགས་ཕྱི་ཐག་ཅན་གྱི་པཎྜི་ཏས། །
འགོ་ཆོས་ཀྱིས་འགྲོ་དོན་ཀུན་མཛད་དེ། །
མ་བཅོལ་གྱི་གླེགས་བམ་བྲིས་དེར། །
བསྟེམ་དམོད་བྱས་པ་ཆ་མཆིལ་ཏེ། །

དེ་ལས་ཀྱང་ནི་ཕངས་སེམས་སྐྱེས། །
རྒྱ་བོད་དག་ཏུ་ཆམས་བསྐོར་བྱས་ཏེ་ཀྱང་། །
སྒྲིབ་པ་དག་པ་མ་ཚོར་དེ། །
ཤེས་རབ་འཕེལ་བ་དངོས་སུ་ཚོར། །

ཚེ་གསུམ་གཉིས་ཟད་པའི་འཇུག་མ་ལ། །
ང་སྒྲུབ་ལུང་ཡོད་ཀྱང་སྤྱོད་ལུང་མེད། །
ངེད་ནི་ས་མཐའི་མི་ཡིན་པས། །
ཡུལ་ཀྱི་དུང་ཀ་སྟར་ལས་ཆེ། །
གྲོགས་ཀྱི་བྱམས་པ་ཅིས་ཡི་གསལ། །
སྤུར་དུ་རང་ཡུལ་འཁོར་འདོད་མཆི། །

Although this is so, thus far it has been my fortune
Not to have suffered from heatstroke.

In an unfamiliar region of a foreign land,
I am like a human deer, without companions.
There are no signs on the roads as to where they lead,
There is no way to know where to stay in this land.

In the early part of my life, I gathered bundles of books;
In the later part of my life, I carried the burden of harsh words.
I have led my life in sorrow;
I wonder if this will serve the teaching of terminology.

But now there is no purpose in speaking words
That have the sharp edge of a rock.
This painful interior, filled with conflict,
Spontaneously emerged to my familiar friends.

My longtime pundit friends
Set out to act for the welfare of all beings.
To the writing of this unrequested book
They may respond with criticism and derision.

More than that, there is a sense of loss;
Although I have gone on pilgrimage to India and Tibet
I have not felt my obstructions being purified,
Though my wisdom has clearly increased.

With two-thirds of my life now gone,
I have the teaching on achievement but not the teaching on conduct.
Because I am a person from a faraway land
My affection for my homeland is stronger than before.
What is it that will show me the love of my friends?
I yearn to return quickly to my own land.[44]

༥༧

ཡུལ་འཛམ་གླིང་ལྗེ་བ་མ་ཧྲཱ་ཧྲཱ། །
རྒྱ་གྲགས་པ་ཅན་གྱི་གཏྲུའི་འགྲམ། །
དུས་དེ་རིང་ཡུལ་བའི་གཏམ་སྙན་ཐོས། །
དུས་ད་ལྷ་མདོ་སྨད་ཤར་ཕྱོགས་ན། །
ལུས་ཞུང་བོ་བསྐྱེད་པའི་མ་ཐན་དང་། །
ལས་སྨོན་པས་འབྲེལ་བའི་སྤུན་ཟླ་རྣམས། །
བདེ་བ་ཙ་བཞུགས་པའི་གཏམ་དེ་སྙན། །

༥༨

ཁྱེད་ངག་ཉམས་འགྱུར་རྫོགས་པའི་གླུ། །
ཐོས་ནས་སྨྱོས་པས་བཟི་བ་ཡི། །
ཡིད་སྨུབས་ལག་པ་ཤོར་བའི་མདའ། །
བདག་གི་སྙིང་ལ་རྣམ་པར་བབས། །

ད་ནི་ཆང་དུག་དྲིགས་ལྡན་མའི། །
གླུ་དབྱངས་སྙན་པོས་ཅི་བྱ་ཞེས། །
གཅིག་ཏུ་ལག་པའི་པདྨོ་ནི། །
བྲང་གི་ངོས་སུ་རྣམ་པར་བྲུམ། །

༥༩

སྔོན་ཚེ་ཀླུ་ཧྲུལ་མདོག་ཅན་མའི། །
སྲིད་པ་ཐ་མའི་ཁྲིམ་བཟུང་བ། །
རྗེ་འཇོག་ཅེས་ནི་བྱ་བ་ཡི། །
གྲོང་ཁྱེར་དེ་ན་བདག་དེང་མཆིས། །

. 45 .

In Magadha, the middle of the land of Jambudvīpa
On the banks of the famous Ganges River,
I heard today good news from home.
I heard the news that today in the eastern part of Do-me
My old mother who gave birth to this body
And relatives connected by my karma and prayers
Are doing well.[45]

. 46 .

Hearing the song in your elegant voice,
The arrow loosed by the god of desire,
Intoxicated with insanity,
Landed in my heart.

Now, what need is there for the melodious tune
Of arrogant honeybees?
The lotus of my palm
Closes at my chest.[46]

. 47 .

Today I am in the city called Taxila
Where in the past
Utpalavarṇā assumed the form
Of a laywoman in her last lifetime.[47]

. ༦༨ .

ཁ་བ་ཅན་དུ་མ་གྲགས་པའི། །
ཁ་གཏམ་འདི་འདྲ་བྲིས་ན་ཡང་། །
ཁ་སླབས་བཟོ་བལྟ་དམན་པའི་ཕྱིར། །
ཁ་ལ་མཉན་མཁན་ཡོང་དོགས་མེད། །

. ༦༩ .

རོ་དང་མཚུངས་པའི་ལུས་པོ་འདི། །
ག་དུས་ཤི་ཡང་མི་འགྱོད་དེ། །
གསེར་དང་མཚུངས་པའི་རྣམ་དཔྱོད་དག།
མཉམ་དུ་ཤི་ན་ཤིན་ཏུ་ཕངས། །

དེས་ན་ཡིད་སྨུག་སྐྱིད་ལུག་དང་། །
ཞུམ་པའི་སྐྱོན་གྱིས་མ་ནོན་པར། །
ཁྱོད་ཀྱིས་འབད་པའི་དགེ་བ་དེས། །
མངའ་བདག་རྒྱལ་པོ་མཉེས་གྱུར་ཅིག།

. ༧༠ .

ལྷུན་པོ་དོ་མཚར་བསྐྱེད་པའི་ཧར་གྱི་གཏམ། །
ཆེན་པོའི་དོ་བསྒྲུང་བརྩེགས་པ་གཅམ་བུའི་ཚིག།
དད་པའི་འཕྲུན་བུ་སློང་པའི་སྒྲུང་གཏམ་དག།
རིང་དུ་སྤངས་ཏེ་དྲང་པོའི་ལམ་དུ་ཞུགས། །

. 48 .

Although I have written this kind of story
About things unknown in the Snowy Land,
Because of my lowly appearance
I need not worry that someone might come to listen.[48]

. 49 .

When this corpselike body dies,
I will feel no regret;
Were these goldlike insights to die with it,
This would be a great loss.

Thus, undaunted by such flaws as depression,
Dejection, discouragement,
By the virtue of your efforts
May the royal lord be pleased.[49]

. 50 .

Empty talk that makes fools amazed,
Fawning words piled up to flatter great men,
Stories that make the faithful sigh,
Leaving these far behind, I set out upon the straight path.[50]

. ༤༡ .

གདུང་བཙུན་བཙུན་པའི་རིགས་དང་ཕལ་བའི་ཚུལ། །
མགོ་རྒྱ་ཚང་བའི་དུས་དང་སྤྲང་པོའི་དུས། །
བཙུན་པ་བཟང་གྲོས་ཁྲིམ་པ་སྡུག་གྲོས་སོགས། །
སྐྱེ་བ་གཅིག་ལ་ལུས་རྟེན་མང་དུ་བརྗེས། །

. ༤༢ .

གཞོན་དུས་དགའ་བའི་ཆུང་མ་ངས་མ་བླངས། །
རྒས་དུས་དགོས་པའི་ནོར་རྫས་ངས་མ་བསགས། །
སྤྲང་པོའི་མི་ཚེ་ལྷུགས་སྐྱུག་ལྷན་ཅིག་ཏུ། །
རྫོགས་པ་འདི་ནི་བདག་གི་སྣང་བ་སྐྱོ། །

. 51 .

A virtuous family, the lineage of monks, the way of a layman,
A time of abundance, a time of poverty,
The best of monks, the worst of laymen,
My body has changed so much in one lifetime.[51]

. 52 .

In my youth, I did not take a delightful bride;
In old age, I did not amass the needed wealth.
That the life of this beggar ends with his pen,
This is what makes me feel so sad.[52]

The Ways of the World

༨༣

ཀ་བ་གདུང་ལྷུམ་བཀྲ་བའི་ཁང་བཟང་གི་དབུས་སུ། །
ཁ་མངར་ཞིམ་དགུའི་ཟས་ཀྱི་མགྲོན་ཁ་ལ་བོས་ཆེ། །
ག་ཡེར་ཡོངས་སུ་སྤྱད་ནས་མགྱུར་དབྱངས་རེ་འཐེན་ནས། །
ང་རང་ཨ་མཆོད་ཆོ་ལས་སྐྱིད་པ་ཞིག་སུ་ཡོད། །
ཅ་ཅོའི་གཏམ་བྲལ་ཁ་ཏོན་དགེ་སྦྱོར་ལ་བརྩོན་བཞིན། །
ཆ་ཡོད་ཡོན་བདག་རྣམས་ཀྱི་ཁྲིམ་ཤུག་ཏུ་འཁྱིངས་ནས། །
ཇ་སོགས་ཟས་གོས་གང་བཟང་ཏབ་ཐོབ་རང་བྱེད་ལ། །
ཉ་འདོན་ཨ་མཆོད་ཚོ་ལ་འགྲན་ཟླ་ཞིག་སུ་ཡོད། །
ཏ་ལེན་ཕྲག་པར་ཁྱེར་ནས་ཡས་མས་སུ་སོང་ཆེ། །
ཐ་ན་དོང་ཚེ་ཇོག་གཅིག་རྙེད་པ་ཡང་དཀའ་མོད། །
ད་ལྟ་ཏ་ནོར་ལུག་གསུམ་ཐོབ་པ་ལ་བལྟས་ན། །
ན་རག་ཨ་མཆོད་ཚོ་ལས་བཙན་པོ་ཞིག་སུ་ཡོད། །
པ་ར་མི་ཏ་ལ་སོགས་གསུང་རབ་ཀུན་སློག་བཞིན། །
ཕ་རོལ་ཡོན་བདག་རྣམས་ཀྱི་མཆོད་ཡུལ་དུ་བཞུགས་ནས། །
བ་འབྲིའི་འོ་ཞོ་བཏུངས་ནས་སྐྱིད་པོ་རང་བྱེད་ལ། །
མ་བཟང་གྲོད་བྲོ་ཟེར་ལ་ཉན་རྒྱུ་རང་ཅི་ཡོད། །
ཙ་རི་དབུས་གཙང་བསྐོར་ནས་ཡོང་ལས་ཤིག་མ་འོང་། །
ཚ་གྲང་བཀྲེས་སྐོམ་མྱོང་བའི་སྡུག་བསྔལ་རང་མཐོང་ནས། །
ཛ་ཡའི་བསྟན་པ་ཀུན་ལ་ཕྱོགས་རིས་ཤིག་མེད་ན། །
ཝ་སྐྱེས་འདྲ་བའི་བླ་གྲྭ་བྱ་བཏང་ཆོས་ཅི་བྱེད། །
ཞྭ་མོ་རྩེ་རྣོ་གྱོན་ནས་གྲོང་ཡུལ་དུ་སོང་སྟེ། །
ཟ་ཆོལ་མཁན་པོ་ཨ་མཆོད་ང་རང་དང་འདྲ་བ། །
འ་ཕུར་དབྱངས་ཀྱིས་ཐར་མདོ་ཤུགས་དྲག་ཏུ་བསྒྲགས་ན། །
ཡ་མའི་བཤད་གཅི་འཆོར་ལ་ཐེ་ཚོམ་རང་ཅི་ཡོད། །
ར་ལྟར་སྐྱོང་བའི་ཨ་མཆོད་འདི་རྣམས་ཚོ་མེད་ན། །
ལ་ལུང་ལྷ་འདྲེ་མང་པོས་སེམས་ཅན་ལ་གནོད་ཡོང་། །
ཤ་ཁྲག་དཀོར་ལ་ཞེན་ཆགས་ཆེ་བ་ཞིག་མ་ཡིན། །

. 53 .

At the center of a good house with beautiful pillars and beams,
When called to a feast of foods of all flavors, bitter and sweet,
Each enjoys it slowly, and then sings a song.
Whose pleasure is greater than ours, the household priests?
Striving at the virtuous practice of recitation, free from chattering talk,
Posing in the inner rooms of the patron's house,
Each vying for anything good: tea, food, and clothes.
Who can rival the household priests at recitation on the full moon day?
When you go up and down, carrying a bag on your shoulder,
In the end, finding even a single coin is hard.
Yet when you see the horses, wealth, and sheep they've gained,
Whose reign is greater than the household priests of hell?
Reciting all the scriptures, like the perfection of wisdom,
You remain recipients of offerings from other patrons,
Each taking delight in drinking the yogurt of cows and female yaks.
What is there to hear but jokes about how bad you are?
Going on pilgrimage to Tsari, U, and Tsang, you saw that it brought nothing
But sufferings of heat and cold, hunger and thirst.
If one has no preference for any of the Victor's scriptures,
What is the use of lamas, monks, and hermits, like predatory foxes?
Going to towns and villages wearing hats with sharp points
The food-seeking abbot is like me, the household priest.
When I forcefully read the *Liberation Sūtra* with thundering voice,
Is there any doubt that Yama will shit and piss?
Without these household priests, rough like horns,
The gods and demons of the passes and valleys would come to harm beings.
It is not out of great attachment to flesh, blood, and wealth,

ས་སྲིད་གང་བའི་འགྲོ་བ་སེམས་ཅན་གྱི་དོན་ཡིན། །
ཏ་ཏ་བཤད་ཚད་ཐམས་ཅད་རྩེད་མོ་རང་ཡིན་ནོ། །
ཨ་མཆོད་རྣམས་ཀྱི་སེམས་ལ་འདི་འདྲ་ཞིག་ཟུངས་ཤིག།

. ༤༨ .

ཀ་ལི་ཀ་ཏ་བལ་ཡུལ་པེ་ཅིང་དང་། །
ཁ་བ་ཅན་གྱི་གྲོང་ཁྱེར་ལྷ་ས་སོགས། །
ག་ས་གང་དུ་ཡོད་པའི་མི་འདི་རྣམས། །
ང་ཡིས་བལྟས་ན་རང་བཞིན་གཅིག་པར་མཐོང་། །
ཅ་ཅོ་འུར་ཟིང་ཕྱོགས་ལ་མི་དགའ་ཞིང་། །
ཆ་ལུགས་ཞི་དུལ་གནང་བ་ཁོང་ཚོ་ཡང་། །
ཇ་མར་གོས་དང་པད་ཤག་མཐོང་བའི་ཚེ། །
ཉ་པ་རྒད་པོའི་སེམས་དང་ཁྱད་མི་འདུག།
ཏ་རེན་སྒྲུ་དྲག་ངོ་བསྟོད་གཏམ་ལ་དགའ། །
ཐ་མལ་མི་རྣམས་གཡོ་དང་སྒྱུ་ལ་དགའ། །
ད་ལྟའི་ཕལ་ཆེར་ཐ་མག་ཆང་ལ་དགའ། །
ན་གཞོན་རྣམས་ནི་མཚོར་སྒྲིག་ཉམས་ལ་དགའ། །
པ་ཕ་ཨ་མའི་ཕྱོགས་ལ་ཞེན་པ་དང་། །
ཕ་རོལ་རིགས་མི་མཐུན་ལ་སྡང་བ་སོགས། །
བ་ལང་དང་ནི་རང་རེའི་མི་རྣམས་ཀྱི། །
མ་བཅོས་སེམས་ཀྱི་རྒྱུ་དག་གཅིག་པར་མཐོང་། །
ཙ་རིའི་གནས་སྐོར་བྱེད་པ་མིང་གི་དོན། །
ཚ་གྲང་དཀའ་ཐུབ་བྱེད་པ་ལྟོ་ཡི་དོན། །
ཛ་ཡའི་གསུང་རབ་ཀློག་པ་ཡོན་གྱི་དོན། །
ཝ་ལེར་བསམས་ན་ཐམས་ཅད་ནོར་གྱི་དོན། །
ཞ་མོ་ཆོས་གོས་བ་དན་སླ་བྲེ་དང་། །
ཟ་རྒྱུ་འཐུང་རྒྱུའི་མཆོད་པ་ཚོགས་འཁོར་སོགས། །
འ་ཅག་རྣམས་ཀྱིས་ཅི་དང་ཅི་བྱེད་པ། །
ཡ་མཚན་ལྟད་མོ་ཙམ་ལས་གཞན་མ་མཐོང་། །
ར་ཁང་ཁྲི་གང་ནང་དུ་སླེབས་པ་བཞིན། །

But for the welfare of the beings who fill the surface of the earth.
Ha ha, everything I've said is but a joke.
Household priests, keep this in mind.[53]

. 54 .

Calcutta, Nepal, Beijing,
The city of Lhasa in the Snowy Realm,
When I look at people wherever they are,
I see they have the same nature.
Even those who don't like chatter and hubbub
And are restrained in their ways,
When they see butter, tea, silk, or money,
Are no different from an old fisherman.
Officials and nobility like flattering talk.
Common people like cunning and deceit.
Today most like cigarettes and beer.
The young like to be pretty and flirtatious.
They keep to their father and mother's side
And hate anyone who is different.
The natural state of mind in humans and cattle
Is seen to be the same.
They go on the Tsari pilgrimage for the sake of their name.
They practice asceticism of heat and cold for the sake of food.
They read the scriptures of the Victor for the sake of offerings.
If we consider it calmly, it's all for the sake of wealth.
Ceremonial hats, monks' robes, banners, canopies,
Ritual offerings of food and drink,
Whatever we do,
I see nothing more than a wondrous spectacle.
Like arriving at a goat shed or a doghouse,

ལ་ལུང་གང་ན་བདེ་སྐྱིད་མི་འདུག་ཀྱང་། །
ཤ་ཁྲག་སྒྱུ་མའི་ལུས་འདི་མ་འཇིག་བར། །
ས་སྙིང་འདི་ཙ་མི་སྡོད་ཀ་མེད་ལགས། །
ཏ་ཅང་དྲང་པོར་བཤད་པ་དེ་འདྲ་སྙེ། །
ཨ་ཅི་གཞན་ཚོ་ཚིག་པ་ཟ་ལས་ཆེ། །

. ༣༣ .

ཞིང་ཆེན་སོ་སོས་བདམས་པའི་འཐུས་མི་ལས། །
ཡིན་མིན་བརྟག་པའི་ཚུལ་བཞིན་འགྲིམ་བྱས་ནས། །
གང་ཞིག་མང་པོའི་ཕྱོགས་སུ་ཐག་གཅོད་པ། །
དབྱིན་ཇིའི་གཞུང་དང་མེ་གོའི་སྲོལ་ལུགས་ཉིད། །

ཡུལ་གྱི་ཡོང་འབབ་གཞུང་ས་ཁོ་ནར་དབང་། །
གཞུང་གི་དབང་ཐག་སྐྱེས་བུ་གཅིག་གིས་གཅོད། །
དེ་ཡི་བསྒོ་བཞག་འབངས་ཀྱིས་བྱེད་པ་དེ། །
ཨུ་རུ་སུ་དང་འཇར་མན་གཞུང་གི་སྲོལ། །

མི་དྲག་མགོན་པོའི་རིགས་ཀྱི་སྡེ་ཚན་ལ། །
ཡོན་ཏན་ཚོད་ལ་དཔག་པའི་གྲལ་བྱས་ནས། །
རྒྱལ་ཁམས་སྐྱི་པའི་བྱ་བཞག་ཐག་གཅོད་པ། །
འདི་ནི་ཤར་ཕྱོགས་ཉི་མའི་ཁབ་ཀྱི་སྲོལ། །

ཕོ་ལུས་ཐོབ་ཆད་རྒྱལ་པོའི་གཡོག་པོ་སྙེ། །
མོ་ལུས་ཐོབ་ཆད་བཙན་པོའི་བཙུན་མོ་ཉིད། །
ཡོད་ཚད་ཐམས་ཅད་རྗེ་ཡི་དཀོར་རྫས་ཡིན། །
ཙནྡྲ་ཤམཤེརམཧཱརཛའི་སྲོལ། ། (བལ་ཡུལ་)

ཐམས་ཅད་ཁོང་དུ་སྦྲིད་པ་ཟབ་མོར་སློམས། །
ཀུན་ལ་དོགས་པ་ཟ་བ་གྲུང་པོར་བྱེད། །
རྙིང་པ་ཐམས་ཅད་ལྷ་ཡི་སྲོལ་དུ་བསྒྲགས། །
གསར་པ་ཐམས་ཅད་བདུད་ཀྱི་འཕྲུལ་དུ་སེམས། །

In all mountain passes and valleys, there is no happiness.
Yet until this illusory body of flesh and blood perishes
We have no choice but to remain on this earth.
A statement like this, so honest,
Alas, may irritate others.[54]

. 55 .

From among the people selected by each state
They proceed, weighing what is right and wrong,
Decisions are made in favor of whoever has the majority.
This is the system of the British and the tradition of America.

The government controls the income of the land.
One man controls the government.
He is appointed by his subjects.
This is the tradition of the governments of Russia and Germany.

Organizing the highest level of the nobility
By measuring their good education,
They decide the affairs of state.
This is the tradition of the Sun Palace of the East [Japan].

All born as males are the king's servants.
All born as females are the monarch's queen.
All that exists is the ruler's property.
This is the tradition of Chandra Shamsher Mahārāja. (Nepal)

Everything hidden within is claimed to be profound.
One who is suspicious of everything is regarded as smart.
Everything old is hailed as the way of the gods.
Everything new is thought to be the conjuring of demons.

ངོ་མཚར་ཕལ་ཆེར་ཐན་ལྷས་ཉིད་དུ་བསྒོམས། །
ཆོས་ཀྱི་རྒྱལ་ཁམས་ཏྲི་ཀྐོ་ཊ་ཡི་སྤྲོལ། །
འདི་ནི་ད་ལྷའི་བར་དུ་རང་རེའི་སྤྲོལ། །
ཀུན་ལ་ཕན་པའི་ངོ་མཚར་རྫས་འཕྲུལ་དང་། །
ཡོངས་ལ་གནོད་པའི་ལྷས་ངན་ཆོ་འཕྲུལ་གཉིས། །
ཤེས་རབ་རལ་གྲིའི་རྣོ་ཕྱོགས་རེ་རེའི་སྣེ། །
གཅིག་གི་ཟླ་ལ་གཅིག་ཀྱང་སླེབས་པར་ངེས། །

. ༤༦ .

དྭངས་གསལ་དྲི་མ་མེད་པའི་རྒྱ་མཚོ་ན། །
ངང་པའི་བུ་མོ་དལ་གྱིས་རྒྱུ་བ་འདིས། །
སྤྲིན་བྲལ་སྔོན་གྱི་ནམ་མཁའ་དྭངས་པ་ལ། །
ཉ་གང་ཟླ་བ་བགྲོད་པའི་མཛེས་སྡུག་འཕྲོག།

རྨོངས་པའི་ཕ་ཤ་ཟ་བའི་དཔའ་བོ་ཡིས། །
མི་འབར་རལ་གྲི་ཕྱུག་ན་འཕྱུར་བ་ལ། །
མ་འཇིགས་སྙིང་ནས་གུས་པས་གསོལ་བཏབ་ན། །
དུག་གསུམ་བདུད་ཀྱི་བུ་ལ་འཇིགས་པ་ཅི། །

གོང་སྟོད་རྗེ་ཡི་གཟུགས་དང་གཡོག་གི་ལུས། །
མཐོང་རྒྱུ་འཁོར་བའི་ཚེ་དང་སྤྲང་པོའི་ཚེ། །
བཙུན་པ་བཟང་ཤོས་ཁྱིམ་པ་སྡུག་ཤོས་སོགས། །
སྐྱེ་བ་གཅིག་ལ་ལུས་རྟེན་མང་དུ་བརྗེ། །

མི་ཡི་མི་ཚེ་ཚེ་ཡི་བྲལ་ཡིན་པས། །
བྲལ་པ་འཆི་བདག་ཡུལ་དུ་མ་འཁྱོལ་བར། །
དགའ་དུས་རིང་དུ་གཏོང་བའི་ཐབས་མེད་ན། །
སྡུག་དུས་ཐུང་དུ་གཏོང་བའི་ཐབས་ཅི་ཞིག།

Most wonders are simply considered bad omens.
The tradition of the dharma kingdom Tibet,
This is our tradition to the present day.
The wonders [of science] that benefit all,
And the magic of bad omens, harmful to everyone;
One sharp edge of the double-edged sword
Is certain to arrive at the other.[55]

. 56 .

In the brilliant, pure, and stainless sea
The leisurely movement of a wild swan
Steals the beauty of the full moon's passage
Across the clear autumn sky, free from clouds.

The hero who eats the flesh of the father, ignorance,
Brandishes a flaming sword in his hand.
If one fearlessly beseeches him with heartfelt respect,
Why fear the son of demons, the three poisons?

The body of the master, the body of the servant,
The life of wealth, the life of a beggar,
The best of monks, the worst of laymen,
Our bodies change many times in one life.

Because the life of a human is the tax of life,
Until the taxed reach the land of the lord of death,
If there is no method to lengthen the time of happiness,
Is there some method to shorten the time of suffering?[56]

. ༤༥ .

སྤྱང་ཀི་ཤ་ཟན་རི་བོང་རྩྭ་ཟན་གཉིས། །
ཟས་ཀྱི་དོན་དུ་གྲོས་ཁ་བསྡུར་བ་ལས། །
རི་ཞིག་རང་རིགས་མཐུན་པའི་འཁོར་ནང་དུ། །
རང་རང་སོ་སོའི་སྤྱོད་པ་བསྐྱངས་ན་ལེགས། །

འབྲོག་པ་རྣམས་ལ་ཕག་ཤ་ཟ་བ་དང་། །
གྲོང་པ་རྣམས་ལ་མར་ཁུ་འཐུང་བ་སོགས། །
མི་འདོད་ནན་གྱིས་བསྐུལ་བའི་དོན་ཡང་མེད། །
འདོད་ན་བཙན་གྱིས་འགོག་པའི་དོན་ཡང་མེད། །

གྲོག་མ་མིག་མེད་བདེ་བའི་ཆེད་དུ་རྒྱུག།
ས་འབུ་རྐང་མེད་བདེ་བའི་ཆེད་དུ་རྒྱུག།
མདོར་ན་འཛིག་རྟེན་ཐམས་ཅད་བང་འགྲན་ནས། །
གཅིག་ལས་གཅིག་མགྱོགས་བདེ་བའི་ཕྱོགས་སུ་རྒྱུག།

སྐབས་འགར་ལྷ་མོ་མཐོང་ཡང་ཞེན་ལོག་བྱུང་། །
སྐབས་འགར་རྒན་མོ་མཐོང་ཡང་ཆགས་པ་སྐྱེ། །
འདི་ཡིན་འཕྲོ་ལ་དེ་མིན་གཞན་ཞིག་འོང་། །
སེམས་ཀྱིས་བསླུས་པ་གྲངས་ཀྱིས་ག་ལ་ཆོད། །

བྱིས་པའི་དུས་ནས་རྒས་ཤིང་འཁོག་པའི་བར། །
སེམས་ཀྱི་ཁྲིར་སོ་ཙི་ཙམ་བརྗེས་གྱུར་པ། །
རང་གིས་མྱོང་བས་དཔྱད་ན་ཤེས་ནུས་པའི། །
ད་ལྟའི་འཆར་སྣོ་འདི་ལ་ཡིད་བརྟན་ཅི། །

རང་སེམས་སྒྲིན་པས་རང་ངོ་མ་ཟིན་པས། །
ཆོས་སྲིད་གནམ་ས་གཉིས་ཀྱི་རྒྱ་ཁྱོན་ཚད། །
རྟག་ཏུ་གཞལ་བའི་འཁྲུལ་སྣང་རིམ་པ་འདིར། །
གཏན་གྱི་སྐྱབས་གནས་བྱེད་པའི་སྙིང་ཁམས་ཅན། །

ཡུན་རིང་འགྲོགས་ན་ཚེ་འདིའི་བྱ་གཞག་ལ། །
མི་སྐྱོ་བྱ་བ་གཅིག་ཀྱང་ཡོད་མ་ཡིན། །

. 57 .

The meat-eating wolf, the grass-eating rabbit,
Instead of discussing the nature of food,
It is best if they kept to their own ways for a while
Within the circle of their own kind.

Making nomads eat pork,
Making villagers drink melted butter.
If they don't like it, there's no point in insisting;
If they do, there's no point in stopping them.

The blind ant runs about for the sake of happiness.
The legless worm crawls about for the sake of happiness.
In brief, all the world is racing with each other,
Running toward happiness, one faster than the next.

Sometimes, seeing a goddess is revolting.
Sometimes, seeing an old woman is arousing.
Thinking, "This is it," something else comes along.
How can the deceptions of the mind be counted?

Our attitudes change so much
From childhood to when we are old and decrepit.
Analyze your own experience and you know this.
How can you have confidence in today's thoughts?

Due to the mind's insanity, we do not recognize our own face,
Yet we constantly measure the secular and sacred, heaven and earth.
Courageous are we who seek lasting refuge
In this series of mistaken appearances.

If we get used to something long enough,
Nothing in this life does not make us sad.

སྐྱོ་བའི་སེམས་གསོ་དམ་པའི་ལྷ་ཆོས་ཏེ། །
སེམས་ཀྱི་ཁོང་དུ་ལན་གཅིག་འོང་བར་ངེས། །

. ༤༨ .

ཕྲག་དོག་ཁྲག་གིས་སྨྱོས་པའི་ཞུ་ཚུགས་སྣག།
འཇིགས་པའི་ང་རོ་སྒྲོགས་པའི་ཚང་ཚིང་ནང་། །
གཅིག་པུར་ལུས་པའི་བདེན་པའི་བུ་ཆུང་ལ། །
ཤེས་རབ་ཅན་གྱིས་སྙིང་རྗེའི་ཡུལ་དུ་དགོངས། །

བླུན་པོ་རང་གི་རྗེས་སུ་མི་འབྲང་ཡང་། །
རང་ཉིད་བླུན་པོའི་རྗེས་སུ་མི་འབྲང་བ། །
དེ་ནི་མཁས་པའི་དམ་ཚིག་དང་པོ་སྟེ། །
སྲོག་ལ་བབས་ཀྱང་འབད་པས་སྲུང་བར་གྱིས། །

. ༤༩ .

གང་དང་གང་ལ་བུང་བ་ལྡིང་འཁོར་བ། །
དེ་དང་དེ་ཙ་རྣམ་པར་གཡོ་བའི་མིག།
དེ་རིང་གློ་བུར་འཇིགས་པའི་བྱེད་ཤ་འདི། །
མི་འདོད་མཛེས་མའི་རྣམ་པར་ཁྱེད་ལ་ཐྲབས། །

དྲི་མེད་རབ་དཀར་ཀ་ཅིའི་ཡོལ་བའི་སྟེང་། །
རྫས་འཕྲུལ་གློག་གི་སྣང་བ་ཁྱབ་བྱས་ཏེ། །
སྒྱུ་མའི་གད་མོ་ཀྲོད་དང་དུ་བའི་གཟུགས། །
སྲིད་གསུམ་འཁོར་བའི་མགྲོན་ལ་ལྟད་མོ་བལྟས། །

གཞན་ཕན་སྙིང་རྗེའི་སྒུམ་དང་བྲལ་ན་ཡང་། །
རིག་རྩལ་ཐབས་མཁས་གློག་གི་ཆོ་འཕྲུལ་གྱིས། །
དྲང་པོའི་མི་ལ་འཁྱོག་པོའི་ལམ་སྟོན་པ། །
སྐྲ་སེར་སྤྲེའུའི་རིགས་ལ་དོགས་ཟློན་མཛོད། །

True divine dharma, solace of this sadness,
At least once, is certain to come to mind.[57]

. 58 .

In the jungle where the frightful roar resounds
Of the stubborn tiger drunk on the blood of envy,
The honest little child is left all alone.
May the wise think of him with compassion.

Though fools may not follow you,
Never follow fools.
That is the first vow of the wise.
Keep it though it costs you your life.[58]

. 59 .

Wherever the bee flies
There the eye moves
Today suddenly this frightening flesh
Engulfs you in the form of an ugly woman.

On a cloth of stainless white silk
Filled with magical electric light
Is the queen of illusion, laughing and crying,
Making a show for visitors of the three realms.

Lacking the oil of compassion that benefits others,
Those skilled in the arts, with the sorcery of electricity,
Show the crooked path to honest humans.
Beware the race of golden-haired monkeys.[59]

. ༦༠ .

མདོན་གྱུར་རྟགས་ཀྱི་བདེན་པ་ངོ་སྤྲོད་ཀྱང་། །
ངམ་ནག་བཞིན་གྱི་གཉེར་མ་མི་སངས་པ། །
མདོར་ན་ཕྲག་དོག་ཅན་གྱི་སྐྱེ་བོ་འདིའི། །
དགའ་བའི་དངོས་པོ་གཞན་གྱི་རྒྱུད་པ་ཉིད། །

. ༦༡ .

ཀ་ན་ཨན་ལྷར་ཡངས་པའི་རྣམ་དཔྱོད་ཀྱིས། །
ཁ་བའི་ལྗོངས་སུ་གསར་འགྱུར་སྤེལ་བ་པོ། །
ག་བུར་འོད་ལ་འགྲན་པའི་ལྷག་བསམ་ཅན། །
ང་ཡི་མཛའ་བའི་གྲོགས་པོ་མཐར་ཕྱིན་པར། །
ཅ་ཅོའི་རྫུན་གཏམ་དེང་སང་ལྷག་པར་འཕེལ། །
ཆ་ལུགས་ཙམ་ལས་མི་ཡི་ལེགས་ཉེས་འཛོག།
ཛ་ཆང་གསེར་དངུལ་ལོངས་སྤྱོད་འཛོམ་གྱུར་ན། །
ཉ་བ་གདོལ་བ་ཡིན་ཀྱང་དམ་པར་བརྩིས། །
ཏ་ལའི་ཤིང་བཞིན་དྲང་པོའི་སྤྱོད་པ་ཡིས། །
ཐ་མལ་ཁྲིམ་མཆོས་རྣམས་ལ་བྱམས་དགོས་ཞེས། །
ད་བོད་རིགས་ཀྱི་སྲས་པོ་མ་ཎི་ཀ།
ན་ཙ་རེད་ཀྱི་སྐྱབས་མགོན་དེ་ཡིས་གསུངས། །
པ་སངས་ལྷ་བུའི་དཔལ་འབྱོར་གང་འཐོབ་ཀྱང་། །
ཕ་རོལ་ཕྱི་མའི་སོ་ཚིས་མི་སྒྲུབ་ན། །
བ་ལང་དུད་འགྲོའི་བུ་དང་ཁྱད་མེད་པ། །
མ་ཎི་ཀ་དང་སངས་རྒྱས་གསུང་རབ་མཐུན། །
ཙ་རི་སོགས་ཀྱི་གནས་ཆེན་བསྐོར་བ་དང་། །
ཚ་གྲང་དཀའ་ཐུབ་སྤྱོད་མཁན་མང་ན་ཡང་། །
ཛ་ཡའི་གསུང་བཞིན་གཞན་ཕན་ལས་བྱེད་པ། །
ཝ་ལེར་བསམ་ན་ས་སྙེང་འདི་ན་དགོན། །
ཞྭ་གོས་ལུས་ཀྱི་ཆ་ལུགས་ངན་ན་ཡང་། །

. 60 .

Though the truth is pointed out with obvious signs,
The wrinkles on a gray face cannot be removed.
In brief, the true joy of this envious man
Is simply the decline of others.[60]

. 61 .

To my perfect friend;
With discernment as vast as Canaan,
Who spreads the news to the Snowy Realm.
With sincerity to rival camphor's light.
The chatter of lies increases these days,
What is good and bad for people comes just from fashion.
When tea, beer, gold, silver, and wealth abound,
Though a person is a fisherman or an outcaste, you consider him holy.
With honest deeds, straight like a palm tree,
Jesus, son of the lineage of David,
Said, "Love the most humble of your neighbors."
This is what the refuge and protector from Nazareth said.
Though one has wealth as great as Venus,
If the housekeeping of the future life is not done,
We are no different from the children of cows.
The Christian and the Buddhist scriptures agree on this.
Though there are many pilgrims to holy sites like Tsari
And those who practice the penance of heat and cold,
A deed that benefits others, in accord with the words of the Victor,
If considered calmly, is rare upon this earth.
Though the style of your hat, clothes, and body is poor,

ཟ་ཀར་ཡ་ཡི་བུ་བཞིན་དྭང་པོའི་ལས། །
འ་ཅག་སྐྱེས་པོ་སྲུ་ཡིས་བརྩོན་ནུས་ན། །
ཡ་ཧོ་ཕ་ཡི་དགོངས་པ་དེ་ལ་མཉེས། །
རྣ་པའི་སྒྲོ་ནས་སྤྲང་པོའི་ཟན་འཚོལ་བའི། །
ལ་ཟར་ཤི་ནས་འཆི་མེད་བདེ་བ་ཐོབ། །
ཤ་ཡི་འདོད་པ་ཁོ་ནའི་རྗེས་སོང་ན། །
ས་དོམ་ཡུལ་དང་ག་མོ་ར་ལ་ལྟོས། །
ཧ་ཅང་གཙོ་བོའི་ཐུགས་དགོངས་མཉེས་པའི་ལས། །
ཨབ་ར་ཧམ་བཞིན་འབད་པས་ལེགས་སྐྱབ་སྟེ། །
ཧ་ཕ་ནས་འོངས་སྡིག་པའི་རྒྱ་མཚོ་ལས། །
ཨ་དམ་བུ་བརྒྱུད་མ་ལུས་ཐར་གྱུར་ཅིག།   ཨ་མེན། །

. ༦༢ .

ཕྲ་ཞིབ་ལེགས་བཤད་སྙན་པའི་ཡན་ལག་ཏུ། །
ངོ་མཚར་གཏམ་གྱི་གླིང་གཞི་ཤེས་འདོད་པའི། །
བློ་གསལ་བློ་གྲོས་འཚོལ་བ་དེ་དག་ལ། །
དགའ་བའི་དགའ་སྟོན་ཉིད་ཏུ་ཅིས་མི་འགྱུར། །

རིགས་གསུམ་སྐད་ཀྱི་འཇིག་རྟེན་ལས་འོངས་པའི། །
རྒྱ་ཆེན་སྔོན་བྱུང་གཏམ་གྱི་གཏྲ་མ། །
རྣམ་དཔྱོད་ཆུ་རིས་ཆགས་པའི་ཡིད་ཀྱི་མཚོར། །
ཐོས་པའི་ལམ་ནས་ཅི་དགར་འབབ་ལ་ལྟོས། །

ཐེམ་པའི་ར་བ་བརྒྱལ་བ་མ་ལྟོས་པར། །
ལྷོ་ཕྱོགས་ཞིང་གི་ངོ་མཚར་ཀུན་མཐོང་བའི། །
བདག་གི་དྲིན་གྱིས་བུ་ལོན་ཁྱེར་ནས་ཁྱེད། །
བདག་ལ་སྐྱུར་ཡང་གཤེ་བའི་བསྡིག་མོ་མཛོད། །

བརྒྱ་ཕྲག་འབད་པ་བརྒྱ་ལམ་ནས་དྭངས་པའི། །
རིགས་པའི་གཅེས་ནོར་ཐང་མར་བརྡལ་བ་འདི། །

Your deeds are honest, like the son of Zacharias.
When he could not be imprisoned by any man like us,
To please the mind of Jehovah,
He died on a mountain seeking beggar's food from a spear
But attained the bliss of immortality.
If you seek only the pleasures of the flesh,
Look at Sodom and Gomorrah.
Deeds that delight the mind of the almighty,
Are accomplished with the effort of Abraham.
May all the children of Adam
Be freed from the sin of Eve. Amen.[61]

. 62 .

For those who seek intelligence and clarity of mind,
Who wish to understand the setting for wondrous speech,
How could the elements of subtle and eloquent expression,
Not be a festival of delight?

The mother Ganges of vast and ancient speech
Comes from the world of the language of the three Vedas.
See how whatever one likes falls from the path of learning
Into the ocean of mind formed from the streams of analysis.

With kindness, I bring to you this loan
Of all the wonders I saw in the south,
Without regard for the wall I had to scale.
In return, you frighten me with abuse.

This vast and precious wealth of reason
Drawn from a hundred paths with a hundred efforts,

མ་མཐོང་གྲོགས་པོ་ཁྱེད་ཀྱི་མདུན་དུ་བདག།
འཆི་བའི་ནང་བར་འཕྲང་བའི་སེམས་ཀྱིས་བསྒྲིང་། །

དེ་ལྟར་ངོ་མཚར་ཀཏྣ་རྣམ་བརྒྱད་ཀྱི། །
བརྗོད་དོན་སྙིང་པོར་དྲིལ་བའི་གླེགས་བམ་འདི། །
གངས་ཅན་ཡུལ་བཞུགས་ཆོས་ཀྱི་གྲོགས་རྣམས་ལ། །
དབུས་འགྱུར་མ་ག་དྷ་ནས་སྐྱེས་སུ་བསྒྲིངས། །

ངེས་འབྱུང་ཟླ་འོད་འཛགས་པའི་ཁ་སྒོ་ནས། །
གཞན་སྐྱོན་སྨྲ་བའི་གློག་གི་ལྕེ་གཡོ་བ། །
ཕྲག་དོག་ཕུང་བོ་གཟུགས་སུ་གྲུབ་འདྲ་བའི། །
མཁས་རློམ་དག་ལ་དོན་དུ་མི་འགྱུར་ཡང་། །

འཕགས་ཡུལ་མཁས་པའི་གཞུང་བཟང་དུ་ཀླུ་ལ། །
ཕྲ་ཞིབ་སྨྲ་བའི་སྦྱོར་བ་ལྷུར་ལེན་པའི། །
བློ་གསལ་ལེགས་བཤད་འཚོལ་བ་འགའ་ཞིག་ལ། །
ཕན་པར་རེ་བའི་བསམ་པ་ཁོ་ནས་བྲིས། །

སྡུག་བསྔལ་རྨི་ལམ་འདྲེན་པའི་མ་རིག་གཉིད། །
བསྒྲིང་བའི་ཐུན་གསུམ་ཅིག་ཆར་རྫོགས་པའི་མཐར། །
གནས་ལྔ་རིག་པའི་སྐྱ་རེངས་འོད་དཀར་གྱི། །
བྱང་ཕྱོགས་ཁ་བའི་འཇིག་རྟེན་མཛེས་གྱུར་ཅིག།

དགེ་བ་འདི་ཡིས་མ་ལུས་སྐྱེ་དགུའི་ཡིད། །
ལྷ་རིག་ནོར་བུའི་དབྱིག་གིས་ལེགས་གཏམས་ཏེ། །
རྒྱ་མཚོའི་སྐ་རགས་འཇིག་པའི་ས་ཆེན་ཀུན། །
ངག་གི་དབང་པོའི་གྲོང་ཁྱེར་འདི་འགྲུབ་ཤོག།

Is sent to the presence of you, invisible friend,
Thinking I will miss you on the morning of my death.

Thus, this book, which distills into an essence
The topics of the eight wondrous kaṇḍa
Is sent as a gift to friends of the dharma in the Snowy Land
From the middle country, Magadha.

It may not be of use to those who claim to be scholars,
Taking the form of a mass of envy,
A tongue that moves like lightning expressing the faults of others
In a mouth dripping with the moonlight of renunciation.

Rather it was done only with the hope of helping
Some with clear minds who seek eloquence,
Who strive to use subtle expression,
Silk brocade, the auspicious texts of scholars of the Noble Land.

The sleep of ignorance brings the dream of suffering.
When the three long watches of the night are complete
May the white light of the dawn of the five sciences
Adorn the world of the snowy north.

By this merit, may the minds of all beings
Be well filled with the riches of the jewels of the five sciences;
May all on the great earth surrounded by the belt of the ocean
Reach this city of the power of speech.[62]

. ༦༣ .

སྔོན་ཆེ་ཀཻ་ལ་ཤ་ཡི་ཕོ་བྲང་དུ། །
ལྷ་ཡི་དབང་པོ་རྟག་ཏུ་ཞི་བ་ལ། །
ཡིད་འོང་ལྷ་མོ་ས་ར་སྭ་ཏི་དེ། །
ཇི་ལྟར་འབྱུང་བའི་ཚུལ་འདི་གཏམ་དུ་བྲི། །

འཇིག་རྟེན་འདི་ན་དགའ་བྱེད་ཡ་ནའི་གཞུང་། །
རྫོགས་པར་བྱེད་པ་ཞི་བ་གཅིག་པུ་ཉིད། །
ཕྱེད་ཙམ་ཤེས་པ་རི་ཡི་བུ་མོ་སྟེ། །
བཞི་ཆ་གཅིག་ནི་ཚངས་པ་མཆོག་གིས་ཤེས། །

རྩོད་པའི་རྒྱུད་པ་ཤིན་ཏུ་མི་ཟད་པ། །
དེ་དག་ཀུན་ལས་སྐད་ཅིག་རྒྱལ་བར་ནུས། །
བློ་ལྡན་གང་གིས་རང་གི་སྒོ་གསུམ་ལས། །
དགའ་བྱེད་སྒྲུ་བཞིན་ལེགས་པར་ཕྱེད་ཤེས་ན། །

གྷུ་ལ་ཡི་དང་བྱང་ཆུབ་ཤིང་དྲུང་དུ། །
ཚོ་ག་བཞིན་དུ་སྦྱིན་གཏོང་དག་བྱེད་ཅིང་། །
ར་མ་ཡ་ཎ་གསལ་བར་བཀླག་གྱིས་པའི། །
བསོད་ནམས་ཕུང་པོ་སུ་ཡིས་གཞལ་བར་ནུས། །

གང་ཞིག་རཱ་མ་ཡ་ཎ་འཛིན་པ་དང་། །
འབྲི་དང་ཀློག་དང་འཆད་ལ་བརྟེན་བྱེད་ན། །
དམ་པའི་སྐྱེས་བུ་དེ་ཡི་འགྲོ་བ་ནི། །
བདུན་གཉིས་འཇིག་རྟེན་དག་ན་སྲོལ་དུ་ངེས། །

གང་ཞིག་དེ་ལྟར་རཱ་གྷུ་ན་ཐ་ལ། །
ཡང་དག་དད་དང་རང་གི་སྒོ་གསུམ་ལས། །
དགའ་བྱེད་སྒྲུ་བཞིན་ལེགས་པར་སྤྱོད་བྱེད་པ། །
སྐྱེས་བུ་དེ་ལ་དགའ་བྱེད་ཉིད་དུ་བསྔགས། །

ས་བདག་ཆེན་པོ་གཞོན་ནུ་འདི་གཉིས་ནི། །
མི་ཡི་དབང་པོ་ཤིང་རྟ་བཅུ་བའི་སྲས། །

. 63 .

I will tell the story of how in ancient times
In the palace of Kailash, the pleasing goddess Sarasvatī
Asked the king of gods, Eternal Peace [Śiva],
How she came to be.

In this world, the scripture *Rāmāyaṇa*
Is known completely by Śiva alone.
The daughter of the mountain knows just half.
One fourth is known by supreme Brahmā.

To be able to conquer in an instant
All the incessant trouble of discord,
The intelligent should know half the *Rāmāyaṇa* well
Through the three doors.

The merit of making ritual offerings
To the Ghula and the Bodhi trees,
And the merit of reading the *Rāmāyaṇa* clearly;
Who can measure the mass of merit?

Whoever keeps the *Rāmāyaṇa* and
Supports those who copy, read, and explain it,
Will be an excellent being in this life
And is certain to create fourteen worlds.

Whoever thus has faith in Raghunātha,
And, through the three doors,
Uses the *Rāmāyaṇa* well,
That being will be praised as Rāma himself.

The two youths, the great lords of the earth,
Sons of the lord of men Dāśaratha,

གཟུགས་དང་ཤེས་རབ་བརྟུལ་ཕོད་མཚམས་མེད་པ། །
རཱ་མ་དང་ནི་ལ་ཀྵ་མ་ཎ་སྟེ། །

ཐུ་བོར་གྱུར་བ་འདི་ནི་ཁྱབ་འཇུག་ལྷ། །
མི་ཡི་གཟུགས་སུ་སྤྲུལ་ཏེ་བྱོན་པ་ཞིག།
གླང་གའི་འཁྲམ་གྱི་སྲིན་པོ་དཔུང་ཚོགས་ཀྱང་། །
འདི་དག་གཉིས་ཀྱི་རྨག་མེད་གཞོམ་པར་བྱས། །

གཽ་ཏམ་བསྟི་གནས་གང་ན་བྲམ་ཟེ་མོ། །
དྲང་སྲོང་དམོད་པའི་རྡོ་ཡི་གཟུགས་བྱས་ཏེ། །
དེ་ཡང་འདི་ཡིས་ཞབས་ཀྱིས་རེག་ཙམ་ན། །
སླར་ཡང་མཛེས་མའི་རང་གཟུགས་ཐོབ་པ་མཐོང་། །

འདི་ནི་ངེས་པར་རྩོད་པའི་འགྲོ་བ་ཀུན། །
འདྲེན་པའི་སྐྱེས་བུ་རྨད་བྱུང་མཐུ་གྲུབ་པ། །
འཛིག་རྟེན་བཅུ་བཞི་ཀུན་ལ་དབང་བསྒྱུར་བའི། །
ར་གྷུ་ན་ཐ་ཉིད་དུ་ཁོ་བོས་ཤེས། །

༦༨

ལོ་ཕྱེད་དག་འདས་པའི་ཡུན་ཚད་དུ། །
ཡུལ་རྒྱ་གར་ཤར་ནུབ་ཀུན་སྐྱུལ་ཞིང་། །
དོན་དགོས་གལ་ཆེ་བའི་ལེགས་སྦྱར་དང་། །
མི་དགོས་ཕྱི་གླིང་སྐད་ཀྱང་བསླབས། །

ས་གཡོན་པའི་ཕྱོགས་ནས་མི་སྤྱོད་ཅིང་། །
བགྱི་འོས་པའི་ལས་བཟང་མི་བྱེད་པར། །
རང་གང་དྲན་ལས་ལ་འཇུག་བྱེད་པ། །
ཁྱེད་ཐ་སྙད་གྲོགས་པོ་ཀུན་ལ་གསལ། །

སྤྱི་སྐེར་གྱི་ཐ་སྙད་སླ་བ་ལ། །
དགོས་དོན་ཕན་པ་ཆེར་མཐོང་ནས། །

Ever controlled and courageous in body and wisdom,
They are Rāma and Lakṣmaṇa.

The elder is the god Viṣṇu,
Coming to appear in human form.
The hosts of demons on the banks of the Ganges
Are utterly destroyed by these two.

In Gautama's abode, a brahman girl
Was turned to stone by the hermit's curse.
When just touched by Rāma's feet,
She regained her own beautiful form.

It is certain that all beings in [the age of] discord
Will attain the power of this marvelous guide.
I recognize Raghunātha alone to be
He who wields power throughout the fourteen worlds.[63]

. 64 .

With the years of my youth passing away
I have wandered all across the land of India, east and west.
I have studied Sanskrit, most useful,
And the useless language of the foreigners.

I did not remain on the left side of the earth;
I did not perform auspicious deeds suitable to do.
I have engaged in whatever action came to mind,
This is clear to you, my sophist friends.

Having seen that there was great purpose and benefit
For the use of general and specific expressions,

དཔལ་དགའ་བྱེད་ཟླ་བའི་གདམ་གྱི་རྒྱུད། །
རྗེ་མི་ལའི་མགུར་འབུམ་ཙམ་ཞིག་བྲིས། །

སྤྱིར་མཁོ་གལ་ཆུང་བའི་ཆོས་ཡིན་ཀྱང་། །
གཞུང་ཆེན་མོ་བལྟ་བའི་གྲོགས་རྣམས་ལ། །
དཔེ་དོན་གྱི་གོ་བ་ཕྲ་མོ་སྟེར། །
ངས་མ་བབས་ཀྱི་འབད་པ་དེ་ལྟར་བྱས། །

ཡུལ་སྣ་ཚོགས་བཀོད་པའི་དཔེ་རིས་རྣམས། །
ལྗོངས་ཁང་ཁྱིམ་སྐྱེས་པ་བུད་མེད་སོགས། །
ཤིང་མེ་ཏོག་ལྗོན་པའི་རིགས་བྱེད་ཚོགས། །
ངས་དཀའ་ཡང་འབད་པ་བརྒྱ་ཡིས་བྱས། །

དུས་ད་ལྟ་ཙི་བཞུགས་ཀྱི་དཔེ་རིས་དང་། །
རྩད་གཅོད་དགོས་པའི་གནས་ཡུལ་ཉེར་བཞི་སོགས། །
བསམས་ན་སུས་ཀྱང་ཤེས་དཀའ་བ། །
དོན་ཆེན་པོའི་མིང་མིན་ཐོ་ཙ་བཏབ། །

གོས་ངན་ངོན་གྱི་སློག་པ་གྱོན་པའི་མིས། །
གདམ་གང་སླས་ཧྲུན་དུ་འགྲོ་ན་ཡང་། །
ཡིད་སྨྲོགས་ལྷུང་མེད་པ་འགའ་ཤས་ལ། །
ཐུགས་དགྱེས་པའི་མཆོད་ཡོན་ཡོང་བར་རེ། །

ཡུལ་འབར་མ་ས་ཡང་སིདྒ་ལ། །
དུས་དེང་སང་སངས་རྒྱས་ཆོས་ཀྱིས་ཁྱབ། །
དེ་ཐམས་ཅད་ཉན་ཐོས་སྡེ་བ་སྡེ། །
གཞི་གྱེས་པའི་རྩ་བ་གནས་བརྟན་ལུགས། །

སེམས་ལྟ་སྒོམ་དབུ་སེམས་སྤྱོལ་ཡང་འཛིན། །
དེ་ཡིས་ཀྱང་ཐེག་ཆེན་བཀར་བརྩི་བ། །
ཆོས་རིགས་པ་ཕྱི་ནང་གཉིས་ལ་སྦྱངས། །
ཕྱི་ཉམས་ལེན་ཚུལ་ཁྲིམས་གཙོ་བོར་བྱེད། །

ཁྱད་པར་དུ་རྡོ་རྗེ་ཐེག་པ་ལ། །
མུ་སྟེགས་ཀྱི་ལུགས་དང་འདྲ་བ་སྡེ། །

I wrote the story of Śrī Rāmacandra,
About the size of the hundred thousand songs of lord Mila.

In general, it is not an essential teaching;
But for friends who read the great texts,
It provides detailed knowledge of metaphors.
I thus made unbecoming effort.

Although it was difficult, with a hundred efforts, I made
Illustrations displaying various lands:
The regions, houses, men, and women,
The various types of wondrous trees and flowers.

If one considers the illustrations of what remains today
And the twenty-four places that must be sought,
It is difficult for anyone to think
That I made a list of unimportant names.

Although men like me wearing simple pelts
Tell lies in whatever they say,
For some, whose minds are impartial,
I hope it will make a pleasing offering.

The lands of Burma, Siam, and Singhala
Are nowadays filled with the Buddha's dharma;
All of the śrāvaka sect,
Split off from the Sthavira school.

In view and meditation they uphold Madhyamaka and Cittamātra.
They even count the Mahāyāna as the Buddha's word.
They study the outer and inner sciences of the dharma.
In outer practice, they place ethics first.

They say that the Vajrayāna
Is like the system of the tīrthikas.

རྒྱུད་སྡེ་མཐོང་ན་ཞེན་པ་བྱེད། །
སྐུ་བརྟེན་མཐོང་ན་ངོ་ཚ་བྱེད། །

དེ་ལ་ཐོས་ཆུང་དགེ་སློང་ཚོགས། །
ཕལ་ཆེར་མཐུན་པར་འདི་སྐད་གླེང་། །
བོད་དུ་ཤནྟ་རཀྵི་ཏས། །
དང་པོ་འདུལ་བའི་སྡེ་བཙུགས་ནས། །
ཅ་ཅོ་མེད་པར་བཞུགས་པའི་ཚེ། །
བོད་མི་མདོ་ལ་ཡང་མ་དགའ། །

དེ་ནས་པདྨ་སཾ་བྷ་ཝས། །
གཏོར་མ་བཤམས་ནས་ཧ་□བརྡུང་། །
སྦྱིན་སྲེག་བྱས་ནས་འཆམ་རྒྱབ་པས། །
བོད་རྣམས་སྔགས་ལ་དད་དོ་སྐད། །

གཞན་ཡང་བོད་ཀྱི་འདུལ་བ་ནི། །
སྲོག་གཅོད་རྫུན་དང་བརྐུ་བ་སོགས། །
གཞན་ལ་གནོད་པ་བྱེད་རྣམས་བཀག།
ཆང་དང་བུད་མེད་ཕྱི་དྲོའི་ཟས། །
ཅི་དགར་སྤྱོད་ཀྱང་རུང་ངོ་ཞེས། །

གཞན་ཡང་ཕྱག་ཕྱ་རིང་པོ་ཅན། །
ཐེག་ཆེན་ལུགས་ཀྱི་ཆོས་གོས་དང་། །
ཤིང་གི་ཕོར་བ་དཎྜ་ཤན་ཅན། །
ཐེག་ཆེན་ལུགས་ཀྱི་ལྷུང་བཟེད་སྐད། །

དེ་འདྲའི་ངེས་མེད་གཏམ་མང་བ། །
བོད་དང་བོད་ཀྱི་གནས་སྐོར་བ། །
སྨྲོ་སྤྱོད་ཅན་རྣམས་དེ་སྐད་སྨྲ། །

དེ་ལ་བདག་གིས་འདི་སྐད་དུ། །
བོད་དུ་བཞུགས་པའི་འདུལ་བའི་ལུང་། །
ཐམས་ཅད་ཉན་ཐོས་སྡེ་སྣོད་ཞེས། །
སྨྲས་ཀྱང་བདེན་པར་བརྩི་བ་མེད། །

If they read a tantra they would be hostile;
If they saw a statue they would be ashamed.

In this assembly of monks of little learning
The majority says this:
In Tibet, Śāntarakṣita
First established the vinaya piṭaka.
When they had to sit without chattering
The Tibetans did not like the sūtras.

Then Padmasambhava
Arranged the offering and beat the horse [text missing]
He made burnt offerings and did the dance.
And so, they say, Tibetans had faith in mantra.

They also say that though the Tibetan vinaya
Forbids killing, lying, stealing,
And doing harm to others
When it comes to beer, women, and evening meals,
Doing whatever one likes is allowed.

They also say that a fox-fur cloak
Is the Mahāyāna monk's robe
That a wooden bowl lined with silver
Is the Mahāyāna begging bowl.

There is much of this confused talk,
Saying that Tibetans and Tibetan pilgrims
Behave in crazy ways.

I say this to them:
"The vinaya scriptures in Tibet
Are all of the śrāvaka piṭaka."
I say this, but they do not think it's true.

ཞིང་ཡུལ་མང་མཐོང་བའི་མིག་འཕྲུལ་དང་། །
ལུས་སྐྱིད་སྡུག་མྱོང་བའི་རྨི་ལམ་དུ། །
ལོ་དགུ་ལ་ས་མཐའ་འགྲིམས་པ་འདིས། །
ང་སྐྱེས་པའི་ཉམས་ཤིག་ཤར་ནས་བྱུང་། །

༨༧

འདམ་བུའི་ཚལ་ན་ཆུ་སྐྱེས་མཛེས་པ་སྟེ། །
ར་རི་ལྷན་ཡང་ཟླ་བ་ཡིད་འོང་ཉིད། །
ཤིང་ཤུན་གྱོན་ཡང་ཕྲ་ལ་ལྷེམ་པའི་ལུས། །
མཛེས་སྡུག་ཅན་ལ་རྒྱན་དུ་མི་འགྱུར་གྲང་། །

ལུས་ནི་མདུན་དུ་འགྲོ་བྱེད་ཅིང་། །
སེམས་ནི་རྒྱབ་ཏུ་རྒྱུག་བྱེད་པ། །
ལྡོག་ཏེ་རླུང་གིས་འཕྱིར་བ་ཡིས། །
རྒྱ་གར་དར་གྱི་བ་དན་བཞིན། །

༨༨

ཁ་རྒྱ་ཀན་རྒྱའི་བར་ནི་རིང་བ་སྟེ། །
དབུས་དང་ཨ་མདོ་ལམ་ཡང་ཤིན་ཏུ་རིང་། །
མ་ག་དྷ་དང་བོད་ནི་ཆེས་ཆེར་རིང་། །
ལེགས་སྦྱར་དངོས་དང་གསུམ་ཀྲང་དེ་ལས་རིང་། །

༨༩

ཟབ་གསལ་ཤེས་རབ་འོད་ཀྱི་འཁོར་ལོས་སྨུན་པའི་འཇིག་རྟེན་འཇིག་པར་མཛད། །
རྣམ་ཐར་ཞི་བའི་ཏིང་འཛིན་ཞབས་ཀྱིས་སྲིད་པའི་རྩེ་མོ་མངོན་པར་མནན། །

Through this roaming to the ends of the earth for nine years
In the illusion of seeing many realms and lands
And the dream of feeling physical pleasure and pain
I feel as if I've been reborn.[64]

. 65 .

In a marsh of reeds, a lotus is beautiful.
Although it has flaws, the moon is pleasing.
Although dressed in bark, what does not adorn
A supple body, endowed with beauty?

My body moves forward
My mind runs behind.
Turning around, I am pushed by the wind
Like a banner of Indian silk.[65]

. 66 .

The distance between a promise and a contract is far.
The road from U to Amdo is very long.
From Magadha to Tibet is most distant.
From actual Sanskrit to Tibetanized Sanskrit is farther than that.[66]

. 67 .

You destroy the world of darkness with wisdom's wheel of light, profound and clear.
You step down upon the peak of existence with the feet of the samādhi of liberation and peace.

སྤྲོས་པའི་སྤྲིན་གྱིས་བསྐྲད་པ་ཡོངས་དག་དྲི་མེད་ནམ་མཁའི་ཐུགས་མངའ་བ། །
དཔལ་ལྡན་འགྲོ་བའི་ཉི་མ་དེ་ཡིས་ཁྱོད་ལ་དགེ་ལེགས་ཆར་དུ་བསྙིལ། །

ཁ་བ་ཅན་ན་སྔོན་གྱི་སྒྲོལ་བཟང་ལས། །
འོངས་པའི་ཡ་རབས་རྣམ་འགྱུར་གང་མཐོང་བ། །
འཕགས་ཡུལ་སྐྱེ་བོའི་སྒོ་གསུམ་ཀུན་སྤྱོད་ཀྱི། །
གཟུགས་བརྙན་འཕོས་པའི་རི་མོ་བཞིན་དུ་གནས། །

དེའི་ཕྱིར་གནའ་རབས་མཁས་པའི་གཞུང་ལུགས་ལས། །
དོན་གྱི་རོ་ཉམས་ཆོར་བ་དེ་དག་ལ། །
ལྗོངས་འདིའི་གནས་ཚུལ་ཞིབ་པར་གླེང་བས་ཀྱང་། །
ཐོས་པའི་ཡན་ལག་རྫོགས་ལ་ཕན་མཐོང་ནས། །

མཐོང་ཐོས་དབང་པོའི་ཡུལ་དུ་མ་གྱུར་བར། །
ཁྲིམས་ཀྱི་མལ་དུ་དཔྱད་པས་མི་ཤེས་པའི། །
ཕྲ་རགས་དོན་གྱི་ཁྱད་པར་ཇི་སྙེད་ཅིག།
རྣམ་གསལ་དཔེ་ཡི་ལམ་ནས་འདིར་བཤད་བྱ། །

. ༦༨ .

རྒྱུ་མཚན་མེད་པར་བརྗོད་ན་ཡིད་ཆེས་ཤིང་། །
རྒྱུ་མཚན་བཙལ་སྟེ་སྨྲས་ན་བརྙས་བྱེད་པའི། །
སྐྱེ་བོ་རྨོངས་པའི་སེམས་ཀྱི་གཤིས་ལུགས་འདི། །
ཚད་མའི་འཇུག་པ་ཀུན་ལས་འདས་པ་ལགས། །

. ༦༩ .

བསྐལ་པར་མི་ཉམས་མཁས་པའི་ངོ་མཚར་གཏམ། །
སྐད་གཅིག་མི་སྡོད་འདུས་བྱས་བསླུ་བའི་ཆོས། །
མཐོང་ཞིང་ཐོས་པའི་རྣམ་པ་ཐ་དད་པ། །
ལྷན་ཅིག་ཚོགས་པའི་སྒྱུ་མ་དེ་ལྟ་ཉིད། །

You are endowed with the mind of the stainless sky, unsullied by clouds
of elaboration.
May that sun, the glory of all beings, rain down goodness upon you.

Whatever expressions of civility are seen
To come from the fine past traditions in the Snowy Land,
Remain like a picture casting a reflection
Of the conduct of the three doors of the people of the Noble Land.

Thus, for those who enjoy the flavors of meaning
From the learned treatises of ancient times,
To speak in detail about the conditions of this land [India]
Might help them complete the branches of learning.

However many things there might be, both subtle and coarse,
That cannot be known through investigation at home in bed
Without becoming objects of the senses of sight and hearing,
I shall explain here using the clearest examples.[67]

. 68 .

If it is said without a reason, one is believed;
If a reason is sought and set forth, one is despised.
This nature of the mind of benighted beings
Transgresses everything that is valid.[68]

. 69 .

Wondrous words of the wise that do not disappear for aeons,
Deceptive phenomena so composed that they do not last an instant,
The difference of what is seen and what is heard,
The illusion that gathers it all together is just like that.[69]

. ༡༠ .

བདེན་པའི་ས་བོན་གནས་པའི་གནའ་བོའི་གཏམ། །
ངོ་མཚར་རི་ལ་མཆོངས་པའི་རི་བོང་རྗེས། །
ཤེས་རབ་མིག་པོའི་ནགས་སུ་བཞུགས་པ་ན། །
འཐད་དང་མི་འཐད་དབྱེ་བ་སུ་ཡིས་འབྱེད། །

. ༡༡ .

དངོས་པོ་རང་འབྲས་འབྱིན་པ་ལ། །
གསོལ་བ་བཏབ་པས་ག་ལ་ཕན། །
མ་ལ་གསོལ་བ་བཏབ་ཀྱང་བུ། །
དུས་མ་ཡིན་པར་བཙའ་མི་ནུས། །

. ༡༢ .

བཙོས་སུ་མེད་ཅིང་བསྐྱུར་རྒྱུ་མེད། །
ལོག་པའི་དཔྱད་ནི་རྫོ་རྗེ་ཉིད། །
སླིན་པ་ལྷུགས་ཀྱི་གདོང་ཅན་ལ། །
སུ་ཞིག་གིས་ནི་ཀྲོལ་བར་ནུས། །

. ༡༣ .

གངས་ཀྱི་སེ་ཏྒྲི་གར་ཡང་མ་མཆིས་ཤིང་། །
གེ་སར་རྒྱལ་པོ་གུད་དུ་མི་བཞུགས་མོད། །
སྒྲོ་བཏགས་སེམས་ལ་དངོས་སུ་སྣང་བ་འདི། །
སྙན་ཚིག་སྒྲ་ཡི་བརྗོད་བྱར་ཅིས་མི་རུང་། །

. 70 .

The old sayings that contain the seeds of truth
The footprint of the rabbit that jumped to the wondrous mountain,
When one enters the forest of faded wisdom,
Who can distinguish right from wrong?[70]

. 71 .

When things bring forth their own effect,
What benefit is there in prayer?
Although one may pray to the mother,
She cannot give birth to the child at the wrong time.[71]

. 72 .

Unalterable and unchanging,
The mistaken crowd is diamond-hard.
Who can possibly argue
With iron-faced fools?[72]

. 73 .

The snow lion does not exist anywhere
And King Gesar does not live elsewhere,
Yet this perception seems so real to the fantasizing mind.
What could be wrong with expressing it in poetic words?[73]

༡༨

ཀ་མ་ལ་ལྷར་ཡངས་པའི་བློ་ལྡན་ཞིང་། །
ཁ་ནས་ལེགས་བཤད་སྨྲ་བའི་སྐྱེ་བོའི་ཚོགས། །
ག་ན་གནས་ཀྱང་ཐ་སྙད་པ་ཡིན་ཏེ། །
ང་ཅག་ཅམ་མིན་མཁས་པ་སྤྱི་ཡི་མིང་། །
ཅ་ཅོ་ཤུར་ཟིང་ཆེ་བ་བདེན་མོད་ཀྱང་། །
ཆ་ཤས་ཕལ་ཆེར་དོན་ལྡན་ཆོས་གཏམ་ཡིན། །
ཇ་བཟང་འཐུང་བཞིན་རྒྱ་བོད་ཧོར་གསུམ་གྱི། །
ཉ་ཉོག་སྐད་ཆ་བཤད་དང་འདི་མི་འདྲ། །
ཏ་ཐ་ག་ཏའི་རྗེས་སུ་ཞུགས་ན་ཡང་། །
ཐ་མལ་ཕྲག་དོག་དབང་དུ་ཆེར་སོང་སྟེ། །
ད་ལྟ་གཞན་སྨོད་ཕྲ་མའི་ཚིག་སྨྲ་བ། །
ན་རག་ཡུལ་དུ་སྐྱེ་བའི་སྔ་ལྟས་ཉིད། །
པ་སངས་ལྷ་བུའི་དྲི་མེད་ལུང་རིགས་ཀྱིས། །
ཕ་རོལ་རྒོལ་བ་འཇོམས་པར་མི་ནུས་པས། །
བ་ལང་ལྷ་བུའི་བླུན་རྫོངས་རྣམས་ཀྱི་ཁ། །
མ་ཤེས་མ་མཐོང་ཚིག་གིས་བརྒྱན་ན་མཛེས། །
ཙ་རི་དང་མཚུངས་གྲུབ་པའི་གནས་མཆོག་འདིར། །
ཚ་གྲང་ཁྲུད་གསོད་ཐོས་བསམ་མ་ནུས་ཀྱང་། །
ཛ་ཡའི་རྗེས་འཇུག་ང་དང་ང་འདྲ་ལ། །
ཝ་མོ་བཞིན་དུ་ཐན་སྐད་མ་སྒྲོགས་ཤིག།
ཞྭ་སེར་བསྟན་པའི་ལུགས་འཛིན་མང་ཐོས་ཚོགས། །
ཟ་འདྲེ་འགོང་པོ་བཞིན་དུ་བརྟས་པའི་ཡུལ། །
འ་ཤུར་□□□
ཡ་མཚན་ཆེ་ཞེས་བསྔགས་པ་སྙིགས་མའི་མཚང་། །

. 74 .

The assembled beings whose minds are open like a Kamala lotus
And who speak well-spoken words,
Wherever they abide, they are lovers of language.
It is not just us; it is a common name for a scholar.
It is true that their noisy chatter is loud
Yet most is meaningful discourse on the dharma.
This is different from the confused babble in China, Tibet, and Mongolia,
Indulged in as people drink good tea.
Although they follow the Tathāgata,
Ordinary people are controlled by envy
Speaking words of slander today, blaming others.
It just foreshadows their birth in the land of hell.
Using scripture and reasoning, stainless like Venus,
They are not able to destroy their opponent.
Thus, the mouths of benighted fools, like cattle,
Are beautiful when adorned with words they have not seen and cannot understand.
Here in this sacred place of adepts, like Tsari,
Scorning heat and cold but unable to study,
I, a follower of the Victor, and those like me,
Pray, do not condemn us, howling like a fox.
To the learned assembly of those upholding the yellow-hat teaching
I am an object of contempt, like a demon or an evil spirit.
The rattle [text missing]
The flaws of corruption are extolled, saying, "How wonderful."[74]

. ༦༤ .

བརྗོད་བྱ་ངོ་བོ་དམན་པ་ཕལ་པའི་རྗོ། །
བརྗོད་བྱེད་མཛེས་པའི་ཚོན་གྱིས་ཁ་བསྒྱུར་བའི། །
བསྟན་བཅོས་ནོར་བུའི་ཟློབ་འདིའི་མཁས་རྣམས་ཀྱི། །
བློ་གྲོས་ཡངས་པའི་ཁང་བཟང་འགྲིམ་དུ་ཆུག།

. ༦༥ .

ཀླུ་པ་ལ་ཡི་སྲུ་བཏོགས་ནས། །
ཁ་ཡི་འགྲམ་དུ་བཙུགས་ཁྲི་འདྲ། །
ག་ནས་འོང་བ་མ་ཤེས་པས། །
ང་ལ་ཆད་པ་མ་གཅོད་ཤིག།

. ༦༦ .

སྐྲམ་ཟུར་བརྒྱུད་འཁོར་ལོ་ཆུང་ངུ་ཞིག།
མི་ཧྲེང་པོ་ཞིག་གིས་བསྐོར་བ་ན། །
ས་དཔག་ཚད་ཉི་ཤུ་ཡོམ་ཡོམ་གཡོ། །
དེ་རྫུན་རྫུན་འདྲ་ལ་མི་མཚར་རམ། །
ཀྱེ་དེ་ཡང་ངོ་མཚར་མི་ཆེ་ཡི། །

ལོ་བརྒྱད་ཅུ་བཀྲལ་བའི་རྒན་པོ་ཡང་། །
ཤ་སྨིན་ཆུང་ཞིག་གི་འདོར་ལེན་གྱིས། །
ལོ་ཉི་ཤུ་གཞོན་ནུར་བྱེད་ནུས་པ། །
དེ་རྫུན་རྫུན་འདྲ་ལ་མི་མཚར་རམ། །
ཀྱེ་དེ་ཡང་ངོ་མཚར་མི་ཆེ་ཡི། །

ཕྱི་འཛིན་མེད་ཀྱི་ནམ་མཁའ་སྟོང་བ་ནས། །
ནང་སྨྱུར་མགྱོགས་ཆེ་བའི་གློག་གི་འཕྲིན། །

. 75 .

The subject matter, a common stone of humble nature,
The expression, a beautiful treatise of changing color;
Allow this fake jewel
To enter the palace of vast learning of the wise.[75]

. 76 .

As if pulling out the hairs of the skull
And sticking them around your mouth makes you look fierce;
Because I don't know where you come from
Don't threaten me with punishment.[76]

. 77 .

A small octagonal box with a small wheel
When spun by just one man
Can tremble the earth twenty yojanas away.
That seems like a lie. Is it not amazing?
Oh, that's not so amazing.

By removing a small scar
An old man of over eighty years
Can be made twenty years younger.
That seems like a lie. Is it not amazing?
Oh, that's not so amazing.

Through the emptiness of outer space
A lightning letter with great inner speed

ས་དཔག་ཚད་ཁྲི་ཙ་འགྲོ་ནུས་པ། །
དེ་རྫུན་རྫུན་འདྲ་ལ་མི་མཚར་རམ། །
ཀྱེ་དེ་ཡང་ངོ་མཚར་མི་ཆེ་ཡི། །

འོད་དཀར་པོ་ཧ་ཛའི་ཉག་འདྲ་ཞིག།
རྒྱང་རིང་པོའི་ཡུལ་ནས་བཏང་བ་ན། །
སྟོབས་ཆེ་བའི་འཕྲུལ་འཁོར་འཛིན་ནུས་པ། །
དེ་རྫུན་རྫུན་འདྲ་ལ་མི་མཚར་རམ། །
ཀྱེ་དེ་ཡང་ངོ་མཚར་མི་ཆེ་ཡི། །

. ༧༦ .

བྱ་བཞག་ཐམས་ཅད་ལད་མོ་སྟེ། །
ལད་མོ་སུ་མཁས་མཁས་ཁྲུར་འཛིན། །
ཆོས་དབྱིངས་ནམ་མཁའི་ཀློང་མཛོད་ལས། །
ཆུ་འཛིན་མཛེས་ཆས་གླུ་ལེན་ཆེ། །

པདྨའི་ལྗགས་བཟང་གློག་དམར་འཁྱུག།
སོ་ཞོའི་ཚིག་ཕྲེང་སྦྲང་ཆར་བསིལ། །
ཕན་བདེའི་ལྗོན་ཚལ་རྒྱས་པ་ན། །
བསིལ་ལྗོངས་བདེ་སྐྱིད་དགའ་སྟོན་འགྱེད། །

སྐར་ཆུང་རྡོ་རྗེ་དབྱིངས་ཀྱི་ལྷོར། །
རྗེ་ཉིད་སྭ་རིགས་ཡོང༷ས་སུ་འཛི༷ན། །
ཤར་ཀྱི་ང་འདྲ་ནུབ་རར་འགྲོན། །
བྱང་གི་ང༷་རྩེ་གུང་ལ་སྐྲིང༷། །

རྗེ་ཡི་ཐུགས་བསྐྱེད་བསམ་ལྷུན་གྲུབ། །
སྤྲེལ་བྱ་ཁྲི་ཕག་དབུས་གཙང་བདེ། །
ཁྲི་ལ་དམར་མོ་བརྫབ་པ་ན། །
གླང་ཆེན་རང་སྟོབས་ཆེས་ཆེར་ངོམ། །

Can travel ten thousand yojanas.
That seems like a lie. Is it not amazing?
Oh, that's not so amazing.

A beam of white light narrow as a single hair of a horse's tail
When sent from a faraway place
Can control a machine of great power.
That seems like a lie. Is it not amazing?
Oh, that's not so amazing.[77]

. 78 .

All activities are imitation;
Anyone skilled in imitation plays the role of scholar.
When a song is sung by a beautiful cloud
From the vast treasure of the sky, sphere of reality,

The red lotus tongue of lightning flashes.
The rain of garlands of words from white teeth is cooling.
When the forest of benefit grows,
A festival of happiness is offered in the Cool Realm.

South of the Vajradhātu temple of Garchung,
The lineage was held for the lord himself.
The great image of the east departed to the west
The northern horn was raised to the sky.

The lord's aspiration was spontaneously achieved.
The monkey, bird, dog, and pig [years] of U and Tsang were happy.
When the red rat fell,
The elephant showed off his great power.

སྟག་གི་ངར་སྐད་སྟོང་གསུམ་ལྡིར། །
ཡོས་རྩམ་ཐག་མིན་ཆུ་འཁོར་རགས། །
འབྲུག་གི་ཁྲི་དཔང་ལྟ་ན་མཛེས། །
སྦྲུལ་གྱི་ཤུན་པ་ཐང་ལ་གཅར། །

ཧ་མཆོག་དང་པ་གསེར་ལྡན་ཆིབས། །
ལུག་གི་ལྷིང་བགྲོས་སྤྲོ་བདེ་སྐྱིད། །
ཕྱོགས་བཞི་འཁོར་ལོ་བཅུ་གཉིས་གླུ།
བྱ་མོས་ལྷག་བསམ་དབྱིངས་ནས་བླངས། །

རྡོ་རྗེ་སྨ་མའི་དབྱངས་སྙན་གྱིས། །
ཟུར་གནས་བློ་ཚལ་བསྐྱེད་དམ་སྙམ། །
རང་གཞན་བག་ཕེབས་གནས་འདོད་ན། །
ཆོས་སྐྱོངས་གླུ་ཡི་ར་མདའ་དྲོངས། །

. ༧༤ .

ཀ་ཡེ་དབྱིན་ཇི་གཞུང་ལ་ཁ་ཙམ་མིན་པའི་སྟོབས་ཤུགས། །
ག་རེའི་དགྲ་ཡི་དཔུང་ལ་ང་ཚོ་ཞེད་དགོས་མ་རེད། །
ཙ་ཙོའི་སྐད་རིགས་མི་གཅིག་ཆ་མཐུན་རྒྱལ་ཁབ་མང་པོས། །
ཛ་ཁྲུ་ཆུ་ཡིས་འདོན་པར་ཉ་ཚོགས་ཐུགས་སེམས་མ་ཕངས། །
ཏ་ལའི་ནགས་ཀྱིས་མཛེས་པའི་མཐའ་གྲུ་སྦྲར་མའི་ཡུལ་ལྗོངས། །
ད་ལྟ་དགྲ་ཡི་ཟུག་རྔུས་ན་ཡང་འཚི་དོགས་མི་ཡོང་། །
པ་ཀྲོད་དཔུང་པ་བཟང་བ་ཕ་རིའི་གཟར་གྱི་དུག་ཆུ། །
བ་བེར་ཞུར་སྦྲུས་འབབ་ཀྱང་མ་མོའི་ཆུ་རྩ་མི་འདུག།
ཙ་རིའི་གནས་ལ་བསྐོར་བའི་ཚ་གྲང་ཐུབ་པའི་མཆེད་གྲོགས། །
ཛ་ཛུས་སྟག་ཤུན་བཀབ་པའི་ཕ་སྐྱེས་དཔུང་ལ་མ་འཇིགས། །
ཞྭ་ལྷར་གཙུག་ཏུ་འཁྱུར་འོས་ཟ་མ་ཏོག་གི་འདོད་རྒྱུ། །
འ་ཚོའི་ཕྱོགས་མཐུན་སྟོབས་ལ་ཡ་དོའི་དགྲ་སྟོབས་མེད་དོ། །
ར་ཙོ་རྗེ་དང་ལྡན་པ་ལ་ལའི་དུད་འགྲོ་མཆིས་ཀྱང་། །

The roar of the tiger thundered through the universe.
The waterwheel was too coarse to crush a rabbit.
The dragon throne was beautiful to see.
The snake shed its skin.

The swanlike supreme horse was the golden one's mount.
The prancing sheep were happy.
This song of four directions and twelve cycles
Was sung by a maiden from the sphere of good intentions.

Through this melody of vajra speech
I wonder whether impartial words were spoken.
If oneself and others wish to remain relaxed
Protect the dharma and support this song.[78]

. 79 .

Oh, the English government possesses a power that is not just talk;
We need not fear the troops of any enemy.
Because many nations with different tongues have united
Fish need not despair that they use water to extract tea from tea leaves.
The country of Burma, a region adorned with forests of palms,
Though tormented by the enemy today, the fear of death does not draw near.
Poisonous waterfall that shows its strength
Though it descends with roaring noise, it has no goddess at its source.
Friends who have braved the heat and cold of the Tsari pilgrimage
Do not fear an army of foxes disguised in tiger skins.
A casket with everything one wants, suitable to be carried on high, like a hat,
There is no power in the enemy that can match the power of our allies.
Although some animals have sharp horns,

ཤ་ཁྲག་མི་ཡིས་སྤྱོད་དུས་ས་ལ་འཛུག་པའི་རྒྱས་འདེབས། །
ཏ་ཏ་གད་གྲོའི་གནས་ཞིག་དེང་གི་དུས་ན་འདུག་གོ།
ཨ་ལ་ལ་ཡི་གྲགས་སྙན་མི་རིང་སྨྱུར་དུ་ཐོས་ཡོང་། །

. ༤༠ .

རྒྱ་གར་རྒྱན་པོས་བསྒྲིམ་པའི་གཡག་རྒྱན་དང་། །
བོད་ཀྱི་མི་ཡིས་བསམ་པའི་ཆུ་སྲིན་སོགས། །
མཐོང་སྙེ་སླ་བའི་གདོང་ནི་ངོ་མཚར་ནོད། །
རྒྱང་རིང་ཡུལ་ན་བཀྲག་མདངས་ལྷག་པར་འབར། །

བདེན་པ་སླ་བའི་ལྕེ་ནི་ངོ་ཚས་ཤི། །
ཆུ་རི་སྐད་གཅིག་ཏ་པ་རྒྱུགས་པ་དང་། །
མགོ་མེད་མི་ཡིས་རྩམ་ཐང་བརྩན་ཚིག་དང་། །
ཆོས་མདོག་སྣ་ཕྲ་སྒྲིག་པའི་ཐུང་བ་སོགས། །

མཐོང་བའི་མི་ལ་ལྷག་པར་རྒྱུས་ཆེ་བས། །
□□□

. ༤༡ .

སྐྱིད་ལ་སྟུག་པའི་འཇིག་རྟེན་མི་ཡུལ་འདིར། །
ཤི་ཡང་ཕྱི་མིག་བལྟ་པའི་རེ་བ་ཡིས། །
སྐྱེ་བོ་ཐམས་ཅད་རང་གི་ལག་རྗེས་ཙམ། །
ཤུལ་དུ་ལུས་པའི་འབད་པ་དང་གིས་བྱེད། །

འདི་ན་འགའ་ཡིས་རང་གི་རྒྱུད་འཛིན་བུ་དང་སློབ་མ་རྗེས་སུ་བཞག།
དེ་བཞིན་གཞན་གྱིས་ལེགས་བཤད་ནོར་དང་སྙན་པའི་གྲགས་པ་ཤུལ་དུ་བཀོད། །
ལ་ལ་འཆད་མཉན་ཆོས་ཀྱི་སྡེ་དང་དམ་པའི་རྟེན་རྣམས་བཞེངས་ནས་འདས། །
གཞན་གྱི་ལག་རྗེས་བསགས་པའི་ནོར་དང་མཛེས་པའི་ཁང་ཁྱིམ་འདི་དག་ལགས། །

When humans use their flesh and blood, they are pinned to the ground.
Today there is a place to indulge in laughter.
Soon you shall hear the pleasing words, "How wonderful!"[79]

. 80 .

Old Indians contemplate old yaks.
Tibetans imagine crocodiles.
Those who describe them from sight might blush.
But in a distant land their luster shines.

The tongue of those who speak the truth dies of shame.
A horseman gallops over a mountain of water,
A headless man drinks thin gruel,
Lies arranged with dyes of five colors.

Because those who have seen such things seem to know more
[The remainder of the poem is missing.][80]

. 81 .

In this world of the human land, pleasing yet painful,
All beings, with a hope that looks to the future,
Naturally seek to leave behind
Some trace of themselves.

Some leave a son or a disciple who bears their lineage.
Others leave behind their eloquence, wealth, or fame.
Some pass away after establishing a monastery or images of holy beings.
The trace of others is the wealth they gathered and their beautiful homes.

ཆོས་ནོར་གཉིས་མེད་སྤྲང་པོའི་ལག་རྗེས་ལ། །
གོང་དུ་སྨོས་པ་འདི་དག་མ་མཆིས་པས། །
མི་ཟས་ཡུན་རིང་ཟས་པའི་རིན་འབབ་ཏུ། །
དེབ་ཆུང་འདི་ཉིད་མི་ཡི་ཡུལ་དུ་བཞག།

མ་བཅོལ་གླེགས་བམ་བྲི་བའི་བྲེལ་ཟིང་གིས། །
མི་ལོ་བཅུ་གསུམ་དལ་གྱིས་ཟད་པ་ལ། །
གཞན་གྱིས་བསྟོད་སྨད་ཅི་བྱེད་མ་ངེས་ཀྱང་། །
གཞན་ལ་ཕན་པ་ཅུང་ཟད་ངེས་པར་མཐོང་། །

As for the imprint of the beggar, lacking both dharma and wealth,
There are none of these things mentioned above.
So to pay for the free meals I ate for far too long,
I leave this small book in a stranger's land.

Through the hectic writing of this unrequested book
That slowly consumed thirteen years of my life,
Although it is uncertain whether it will be praised or blamed by others,
I see that it is certain to be of some small benefit to others.[81]

Songs of the Tibetan Kings

. ༧༢ .

འདྲེན་པ་འགྲོ་བའི་ལེགས་བྱས་ལོ་མའི་མཚོར། །
དགྱེས་པའི་ཐ་རླབས་འཁྱིལ་བའི་ཞལ་སྒོ་ནས། །
ཟླ་བའི་མདངས་ལྡན་ཐགས་བཟང་བཞི་བཅུའི་ཚོམས། །
འཛུམ་པའི་འོད་ཀྱིས་ཁྱེད་ལ་སྣང་གྱུར་ཅིག།

རིགས་ཀྱི་སྲུ་ཧྲིག་ཆེ་བའི་འོད་ལྡན་འོད་གསལ་ལྷ་ཡི་གདུང་རྒྱུད་འཛིན། །
སྲེ་བཞིའི་ལྷུན་ཆགས་སྲིད་ཀྱི་གངས་རི་གངས་ཅན་དབུས་ན་མཐོ་བར་བྱས། །
བཀའ་ཡིས་བསྐྱངས་པའི་འབངས་ཀྱི་བདེ་སྐྱིད་བདེ་ལྡན་ཞིང་གི་རྗེས་འགྲོར་མཛད། །
ཀུན་རིག་འཕྲུལ་མངའ་སྲིད་པའི་སེམས་པོ་སེམས་དཔོན་རྣམ་གསུམ་རྒྱལ་གྱུར་ཅིག།

ལྷ་གཅིག་ཕྱག་ན་པདྨོ་མི་རྗེའི་ཚུལ། །
ལུགས་གཉིས་འཁོར་ལོ་བསྒྱུར་བའི་དབང་ཕྱུག་ཆེ། །
སྲིད་གསུམ་ཟིལ་གནོན་སྲོང་བཙན་སྒམ་པོ་ཡིས། །
མཐའ་བཞིའི་རྒྱལ་ཁམས་དབང་དུ་བསྡུས་པའི་ཚུལ། །

ངེས་པའི་སྒྲོས་དང་གསལ་བའི་ལོ་ཚིགས་སུ། །
བཀོད་པའི་ཡིག་རྙིང་ཇི་སྙེད་བསྒྲིགས་པ་ལས། །
བོད་ཁམས་དང་པོའི་སྲིད་དང་དབང་གི་ཚད། །
ཅུང་ཟད་འཇལ་བའི་སྤོབས་པ་བདག་ལ་སྐྱེས། །

སྙིང་སྟོབས་དགུ་འགྱུར་སྲོག་གི་དབྱུག་པ་ལ། །
རྟ་མཆོག་ཁྲིམས་པའི་བཀའ་ཡི་རྒྱས་བཏབ་པའི། །
སྲིན་པོ་གདོང་དམར་བོད་ཀྱི་དམག་དཔུང་གིས། །
སུམ་ཉིས་ས་ཡི་དཀྱིལ་འཁོར་བཟུང་ཞེས་གྲགས། །

. 82 .

From the mouth of the Guide flow waves of joy
Into the ocean of milk, good fortune of migrators.
Protect us with the light of your smile
Of forty perfect teeth, bright as the moon.

The descendants of the gods of clear light, endowed with the light of the lineage's great pearl,
Ascending to the snowy midst of snowy mountains, dazzling realm of the four domains,
Your happy subjects, protected by your word, followed you to a happy land.
May the three ancestral kings, patriarchs of the realm, prevail, endowed with the magic power of all knowledge.

How the one god Padmapāṇi, in the form of the lord of humans,
The great god, turned the wheel of the two systems;
How Song-tsen gam-po, outshining the three worlds,
Brought the kingdoms in the four directions under his rule.

Compiling the available ancient writings
Setting forth authentic accounts and clear chronologies,
I have mustered a small degree of courage
To measure the breadth and might of the first Tibetan realm.

It is said that Tibet's army of red-faced demons,
Pledging their lives with growing courage
To the command of the wrathful Hayagrīva,
Once conquered two-thirds of the earth's circle.[82]

. ༨༣ .

ལྷན་གཅིག་སྐྱེས་པའི་གངས་ཀྱི་སྤུ་ཕྱེད་ལ། །
ལུགས་གཉིས་ཐབས་ཤེས་དུང་གི་མཁར་བསྐྱིལ་པའི། །
རིགས་གསུམ་མགོན་པོས་སྐྱུལ་པའི་རྒྱལ་ཁམས་འདིའི། །
ཕྱོགས་བཞིའི་རྒྱ་ཁྱོན་སུ་ཡིས་འཇལ་བར་ནུས། །

. ༨༤ .

འདི་ནི་རང་བྱུང་བདེན་པའི་ཟླ་བ་སྟེ། །
སྐྱོན་མེད་དུང་གི་ཁ་དོག་གསལ་བ་ལ། །
ཕྱོགས་ལྷུང་ལར་རྒྱའི་རྣ་བ་རིང་བ་ཡི། །
མི་སྨུག་རི་བོང་གཟུགས་དེ་ཅི་ལ་བྲི། །

. ༨༥ .

གཡོ་མེད་སྙིང་རྗེའི་དབང་ཕྱུག་སྤྱན་རས་གཟིགས། །
ཡུད་ཙམ་ཁྲོས་པའི་སྤྱན་གྱི་སྟང་མིག་གིས། །
གསེར་འབྲུག་སྟེར་ལྷའི་ཁྲི་ལ་འཁྱིངས་པ་ཡི། །
མཐུ་ལྡན་གནམ་གྱི་བུ་ཡང་འདར་བར་བྱས། །

. ༨༦ .

མི་བཟད་དགུན་གྱི་རླུང་དང་ལྷན་ཅིག་ཏུ། །
མི་སྨུག་ཁ་བའི་ཡུལ་ནས་ཕྱིར་འཐོན་པའི། །
མི་ཐུབ་སེང་གེ་དཀར་མོའི་དམག་དཔུང་ལ། །
མི་ཡི་དབང་པོ་འཇིགས་པ་ཅིས་མི་བདེན། །

. 83 .

In the Ring of Snows, created at once,
A castle of conch was built by the two ways: method and wisdom.
This kingdom emanated by the three lineages' protectors;
Who can measure its extent in the four directions?[83]

. 84 .

This is the self-arisen moon of truth
Untainted and clear, the color of conch.
Why would one draw an ugly rabbit on it
With the long ears of bias?[84]

. 85 .

Avalokiteśvara, unwavering lord of compassion,
At the wrathful glance of your instantly angered eye,
Even the mighty Son of Heaven
Trembles on the throne of the five-clawed golden dragon.[85]

. 86 .

Emerging from the unbeautiful Land of Snows
With the unbearable wind of winter
Come the unbeatable troops of white lions.
How could the Lord of Men's fear be untrue?[86]

༼ ༤༣ ༽

རང་སྙིའི་རིགས་ལ་ཞེན་པ་དཀར་པོའི་མདངས། །
རང་བྱུང་སྙིང་གི་དབུས་ན་གནས་པ་འདིས། །
རང་ཡུལ་ཁ་བ་ཅན་གྱི་རྫེ་འབངས་ལ། །
རང་གིས་ནུས་པའི་སྲི་ཞུ་ཅུང་ཟད་སྒྲུབ། །

༼ ༤༤ ༽

ཕྱོགས་ལྷུང་ཞེན་པས་དམར་པོར་མ་བྱས་ཤིང་། །
ངོ་བསྟུང་ཚིག་གིས་སྔོན་པོར་མ་བྱས་ལ། །
ཕྱིས་བྱུང་གཏམ་གྱིས་སེར་པོར་མ་བྱས་པ། །
དེ་ཕྱིར་འདི་ནི་དེབ་ཐེར་དཀར་པོ་ཡིན། །

སྙིང་སྟོབས་དགུ་འགྱུར་སྲོག་གི་དབྱུག་པ་ལ། །
རྟ་མཆོག་ཁྲིས་པའི་བཀའ་ཡིས་རྒྱས་བཏབ་པའི། །
སྲིན་པོ་གདོང་དམར་བོད་ཀྱི་དམག་དཔུང་གིས། །
སུམ་གཉིས་ས་ཡི་དཀྱིལ་འཁོར་བཟུང་ཞེས་གྲགས། །

ལྷ་གཅིག་ཕྱག་ན་པདྨ་མི་རྗེའི་ཚུལ། །
ལུགས་གཉིས་འཁོར་ལོ་བསྒྱུར་བའི་དབང་ཕྱུག་ཆེ། །
སྲིད་གསུམ་ཟིལ་གནོན་སྲོང་བཙན་སྒམ་པོ་ཡིས། །
མཐའ་བཞིའི་རྒྱལ་ཁམས་དབང་དུ་འདུས་པའི་ཚུལ། །

ཞིབ་མོའི་ལོ་ཚིགས་བཅད་པའི་རྒྱལ་རབས་སུ། །
བཀོད་པའི་ཡིག་རྙིང་ཅི་སྙེད་བསྒྲིགས་པ་འདིས། །
སྤྱར་རྒྱལ་གོང་མའི་སྲིད་དང་དབང་གི་ཚད། །
ཅུང་ཟད་འཛལ་བའི་སྤོབས་པ་བདག་ལ་སྐྱེས། །

ཤིན་ཏུ་ཡིད་འཕྲོག་བདེན་པའི་བཞིན་རས་ལ། །
མི་གསལ་ཚིག་གི་སེང་རས་གཡོགས་པ་འདི། །

. 87 .

With the luster of white loyalty to my race
Abiding in the center of my self-arisen heart
I have rendered a small service with my strength
To the king and his subjects of my snowy land.[87]

. 88 .

Not made red with bias,
Not made blue with fawning words,
Not made yellow with talk of the future,
This, therefore, is the white annals.

It is said that Tibet's army of red-faced demons,
Pledging their lives with growing courage
To the command of the wrathful Hayagrīva,
Once conquered two-thirds of the earth's circle.

How the one god Padmapāṇi, in the form of the lord of humans,
The great god, turned the wheel of the two systems;
How Song-tsen gam-po, outshining the three worlds,
Brought the kingdoms in the four directions under his rule.

Compiling the available ancient writings
Set forth in royal chronicles with detailed dates
I have mustered a small degree of courage
To measure the breadth and might of the ancient realm of Pur.

This most enchanting face of truth
Is covered with a veil of unclear words.

དཔྱད་གསུམ་སོར་མོས་དུམ་བུར་རལ་བ་ཡི། །
མི་བསྣུན་མཁས་པའི་ཐོ་ཅོ་ཁོ་བོས་བྱས། །

ངོ་མཚར་གཏམ་གྱིས་ཁ་དོག་མ་བསྒྱུར་བའི། །
བདེན་པའི་ནོར་བུ་རྗེན་པར་མཐོང་བ་ན། །
བྱིས་པའི་སྐྱེ་བོས་མཚར་དུ་མི་འཛིན་ཀྱང་། །
ལེགས་པའི་རིན་ཐང་རང་གི་ཁོང་ན་གནས། །

མངའ་བདག་ལྷ་ཡི་མཛད་པའི་དབང་ཐང་དང་། །
རྒྱལ་རབས་བརྒྱུད་ཀྱི་ལོ་ཁམས་གུང་བསྒྲིགས་ནས། །
ཚུལ་གསུམ་རྩིས་ལ་བབས་པའི་བག་མ་འདི། །
གཞུར་གནས་མཁས་པའི་བུ་ལ་ནན་གྱིས་སྤྲིན། །

གཞུར་གནས་རྣམ་པར་དཔྱོད་པའི་ནམ་མཁའ་ལ། །
ཕྱོགས་དང་རིས་ཀྱི་སོ་མཚམས་མ་མཆིས་ཏེ། །
དྭངས་པའི་རང་མདངས་དཀར་བའི་སེམས་ཀྱི་སྤྲིན། །
དུང་སེམས་འོ་མའི་ལྷུ་བ་འཁྲིག་པའི་སྤྲིན། །
རང་སྟེ་ཁ་བ་རི་ཡི་ཕྱོགས་སུ་སོང་། །

ང་རྒྱལ་འབྱུང་པོ་ལངས་པའི་གྲིབ་མ་དང་། །
ཕྲག་དོག་འདྲེ་མོ་དུ་བའི་འོ་དོད་ལ། །
དགོས་མེད་རིག་པ་རིང་དུ་འདྲིས་པའི་དབྱིངས། །
ད་ནི་བདག་ལ་འཛིགས་པའི་འདུ་ཤེས་ཟད། །

ཚེ་གཅིག་ཡུལ་ལ་གནས་པའི་མི་ཆོས་དང་། །
དོན་གཉིས་འབྲས་བུ་སྨྲོལ་བའི་ཆོས་ཁྲིམས་དེ། །
དུས་གསུམ་ཀུན་ཏུ་བདེ་དགའི་དཔལ་སྤྲིན་པས། །
སྡེ་བཞིའི་ནོར་གྱིས་བོད་ཁམས་འཕྱུར་བུ་བྱས། །

ས་ལ་འཁྱིལ་བའི་འབྲུག་གི་སྐྱུག་པ་ཡི། །
ཆུ་བོའི་གཏེར་ཁ་ལྷ་བུའི་དམག་སྡེ་དག།
མེ་ཡིས་ཨག་ཆོམ་འབར་བས་སྐམ་པ་ན། །
ལྷུང་གི་རྒྱལ་མཚན་ཚངས་པའི་ཟློལ་དུ་འཁྲིག།

The senseless talk of me, unruly scholar,
Has torn it with the nails of three analyses.

When one sees nakedly the jewel of truth,
Its color unchanged by fanciful words,
Though childish beings may not find it wondrous,
The value of its excellence lies within.

Comparing the domains made by divine monarchs
As well as dates in royal chronicles,
This bride, based on three methods of calculation,
Is insistently offered to impartial scholars' sons.

In the sky of impartial analysis
No lines divide region and clan;
Clouds of mind, naturally white, reflect its clarity.
Dense clouds, forming the milk of affection,
Went toward their own domain, the mountains of snow.

The shadow of the looming ghost of pride,
The wailing of the weeping witch of envy,
The realm of long-familiar useless knowledge;
Now my sense of fear is finished.

With the ways of humans, lasting for the length of one life,
And the code of the dharma, bearing the fruit of the two goals,
Bestowing the glory of joy in all three times,
The realm of Tibet flowed with fourfold wealth.

The vomit of the dragon that swirls on the earth,
The troops like the treasure in that liquid;
When roasted by burning the beard with fire,
The banner of wind forms in the guise of steam.

དུས་གསུམ་དུས་ཀྱི་འཁོར་ལོ་འཁོར་བ་ན། །
བྱུང་ནས་ཡལ་བའི་སྔོན་གྱི་གཟུགས་བརྙན་རྣམས། །
སྣོད་པའི་དབྱིངས་ལ་སེམས་ཀྱིས་བྲིས་པ་འདི། །
འདས་པའི་འཇིག་རྟེན་མཚོན་པའི་འདྲ་འབག་ཉིད། །

ཟོལ་གྱིས་བཅོས་པའི་སྙིན་མ་མི་གཡོ་ཞིང་། །
སྒྱོགས་སུ་ལྷུང་བའི་ཟུར་མིག་མི་བལྟ་ཡང་། །
རང་བཞིན་གཤིས་ཀྱིས་འཛུམ་པའི་མེ་ཏོག་འདིས། །
དམྱོད་ལྡན་སྐྱེ་བོའི་ཡིད་དབང་ཅིས་མི་འཕྲོག།

མི་ཐུབ་དཔའ་བོའི་རྩལ་གསུམ་རྫོགས་པ་ན། །
མི་བཟད་ཁ་བའི་འབེན་གྱིས་མ་ཁེགས་པའི། །
མི་འཇིགས་སེང་གེ་དཀར་མོའི་དམག་སྡེ་ལ། །
མི་ཡི་རྗེ་བོ་སྤྲངས་པ་ཅིས་མི་བདེན། །

དེ་རིང་མི་མཐོང་འདས་པའི་གཞོན་ནུ་ནམ་ཡང་རྒ་བ་ཡོད་མིན་ཏེ། །
ད་དུང་མ་སླེབས་ཕྱིས་ཀྱི་ན་ཆུང་རྟག་ཏུ་དར་མི་ཆོ་ལ་གནས། །
ད་ལྟ་སྐྱེས་པའི་རྟོག་པའི་ཁྱིམ་ན་དེ་གཉིས་ལྷན་ཅིག་འཛོམས་པ་འདི། །
ཁམས་གསུམ་འགྲོ་བའི་སྐད་དུ་བྲིས་པའི་ལོ་རྒྱུས་ཀུན་གྱི་ས་བོན་ཉིད། །

དེས་ན་གཞི་མེད་སེམས་ཀྱི་སྣོད་གཟུགས་ལ། །
སྣ་ཚོགས་ཚིག་གི་ཚོན་གྱིས་ལེགས་སྤྲས་ཏེ། །
གདོས་བཅས་དངོས་པོའི་གྲལ་དུ་བཞག་པ་འདི། །
ཤིན་ཏུ་ངོ་མཚར་སྒྱུ་མའི་དེབ་ཐེར་ལགས། །

དྲེགས་ལྡན་ཚུག་པ་ཁྲོས་པའི་ཏ་ཏ་དང་། །
བླུན་པོ་ཕག་གིས་བརྟྲས་པའི་ཏུམ་སྒྲ་དང་། །
བློ་ཆུང་བྱིས་པ་དགོད་པའི་སྣ་གཉེར་ལ། །
འཇིགས་པའི་ཡ་ང་བདག་ལ་ཡོད་མ་ཡིན། །

ཕྱོགས་རིས་འཕྱེ་བོས་འགྲོས་ཀྱི་སྒྱུ་རྩལ་དང་། །
འདི་ནང་གཅིག་པོར་མཐོང་བའི་མིག་སྟོང་ལས། །

When the wheel of time turns through three ages,
The reflections of the past rise and fade away.
What was written by the mind in the empty sphere
Is a mask that shows a bygone world.

Not arching eyebrows drawn with cunning,
Not casting sidelong glances of bias,
Why would this flower that blooms so naturally
Not enchant the mind of a discerning person?

When the triple skills of the unconquerable hero are complete
The unfrightened troops of white lions
Are unimpeded, though the target of unbearable snow.
How could the Lord of Men's terror be untrue?

In the youth of the past, unseen today, there is no aging.
The maiden of the future, still unarrived, lives a human life, ever young.
The meeting of those two in the house of thoughts produced in the present:
This is the seed of all histories in the voices of migrators in the three realms.

Thus, in the empty form of the mind without foundation
Well adorned with the colors of various words
This that is placed in the category of a material thing
Is a most wondrous magical chronicle.

The angry *ha ha* of arrogant owls
The abusive *hum* of stupid pigs
The wrinkled nose of small-minded fools' giggles,
For these I have no anguish of fear.

Free from walking with the limp of bias,
And the hostile glance that sees but one thing there,

ལྷུན་པོའི་མལ་ནས་མགྲིན་པ་འདེགས་བཞིན་དུ། །
ཕྱོགས་མེད་དཔྱོད་ལྡན་སེམས་ལ་འཇིགས་པ་བྲལ། །

༤༩

གཏུམ་དྲག་དཔའ་བོའི་སྙིང་རྩ་འདར་བྱེད་པའི། །
གདོང་དམར་དམག་གི་ཀྱཻ་སྒྲ་གསན་པ་ན། །
གནམ་གྱིས་བསྐོས་པའི་ས་ཡི་ཚངས་པ་ཡང་། །
གཡོ་མེད་གསེར་གྱི་ཁྲི་ལས་གཞོལ་ཏེ་བྲོས། །

དོན་ཆུང་རྣམ་རྟོག་བྲག་གི་སྲིན་མོའི་ཁྲག།
གཞུང་བཟང་སྤྲེའུའི་རུས་ལ་ཐིམ་པ་ཡིས། །
བཟང་ངན་རིགས་གཉིས་འདྲེས་པའི་བོད་ཀྱི་མི། །
གདོན་གཟུགས་བོན་པོའི་མོ་ཡིས་བསླུས་པར་ཟད། །

ལྷུན་པོའི་འགོ་མཐུག་ཆེག་གི་གྲལ་རིམ་ཞིག།
མགྲིན་བཟང་ཡིད་གཞུང་ཚོགས་ཀྱི་དབུས་ན་བརྗོད། །
སྙིང་རྗེས་བསྐྱུལ་བའི་འཇུམ་བག་ཅུང་ཟད་སྟུ་ལ། །
དགྱེས་པའི་མགྲོན་པོ་ཅི་ཡང་འབོད་མ་ནུས། །

Raising my voice from the seat of a fool,
The mind of impartial analysis is fearless.[88]

. 89 .

When they hear the red-faced army's battle cry "*kwi*"
Rattling the heart of a fierce and wrathful hero,
Even Brahmā of the earth, appointed by heaven,
Descends from his stable golden throne and flees.

Thoughts of little meaning, the blood of a rock ogress,
Dissolved in good scriptures, the bone of the monkey.
Thus, the people of Tibet, a mix of two lineages, good and evil,
The demon was deceived by Bon po divination.

The sequence of the opening and closing words of a fool
Are expressed amidst the assembly of the eloquent.
Please bestow a small smile inspired by compassion;
I dare not invite a guest who would be pleased.[89]

Precepts on Passion

. ༢༠ .

གལ་ཏེ་འཁྲིག་པའི་འབྲེལ་བས་མ་བསྡུས་ན། །
ཕོ་མོའི་རིགས་ན་འདི་ལྟར་ཐ་དད་པས། །
འཇིག་རྟེན་ཁམས་སུ་སྡེ་གཉིས་ཆད་གྱུར་ཏེ། །
རྟག་ཏུ་གཡུལ་དང་རྩོད་པས་གནས་པར་ངེས། །

. ༢༡ .

འཁྲིག་པ་སྤངས་ན་མི་ཡི་འཇིག་རྟེན་ཁམས། །
སྐད་ཅིག་ཙམ་ལ་ངེས་པར་སྟོང་འགྱུར་ཞིང་། །
མི་ཡི་སེམས་ཅན་མེད་ན་དགེ་སློང་དང་། །
སངས་རྒྱས་བསྟན་པ་དེ་ལས་ག་ལ་འོང་། །

. ༢༢ .

ཨ་ཙང་ཁོ་བོ་དེང་སང་སྨྲོན་པ་སྟེ། །
མ་སྨྲོས་པ་རྣམས་བཞད་གད་བྱེད་ཀྱང་འཚལ། །
བདེ་བ་སྦྱོང་བ་དེ་ཡང་དོན་ཆུང་མིན། །
རིགས་བརྒྱུད་བསྐྱེད་པ་དེ་ཡང་དོན་ཆུང་མིན། །
བདེ་སྟོང་དང་ནས་ཆགས་ལམ་སྐྱོང་ནུས་ན། །
དེ་ལས་ཀྱང་ནི་དོན་ཆུང་ག་ལ་ཡིན། །

. ༢༣ .

སྙིང་ཆུང་རྐུན་པོས་ཁ་ཟས་ཟ་བ་བཞིན། །
སྨུན་པའི་མལ་དུ་སྒྲ་མེད་དལ་བུ་ཡིས། །

. 90 .

Because men and women are so different,
If they were not joined by coupling,
The world would be split into two factions
Always in quarrels and war.[90]

. 91 .

If coupling was abandoned in the realm of humans,
It would surely become empty in an instant.
And if there were no human beings
How could there be monks and the Buddha's teachings?[91]

. 92 .

Of course, these days I am a madman.
Those who are not mad might wish to laugh.
But the experience of bliss is not of small meaning;
The creation of families is not of small meaning.
To sustain the path of passion in a state of bliss and emptiness,
How could that be of small meaning?[92]

. 93 .

Like a timid thief eating a meal in hiding,
To churn in and out and then ejaculate

བསྒྲུབ་ཅིང་ཁྲུ་བ་འཁྱིན་པ་ཙམ་ཞིག་གིས། །
ཆགས་པའི་དགའ་སྟོན་ཡོངས་སུ་རྫོགས་མ་ཡིན། །

དེ་ཕྱིར་ཆགས་ལྡན་སྐྱེས་བུ་ཕོ་མོ་ལ། །
བུ་རམ་འོ་མ་སྦྲང་རྩིའི་རོ་བཞིན་དུ། །
མི་འདྲ་སྣ་ཚོགས་བདེ་བའི་རོ་སྨིན་པའི། །
འདོད་པའི་སྒྱུ་རྩལ་དྲུག་ཅུར་ཤེས་པར་བྱ། །

. ༤༨ .

ཐོག་མར་དཔུང་པ་དེ་ནས་མཆན་ཁུང་དང་། །
དེ་ནས་དཔལ་གྱིས་ལྟེ་བར་འོ་བྱེད་ཅིང་། །
ལྷག་པར་སྨྱོས་ནས་བརླ་དང་ལྟ་ག་སྟེ། །
ཡུར་བའི་ཆུ་ཕྲན་མཚོ་ལ་དྲངས་པར་བྱ། །

. ༤༩ .

འདྲིས་ཤིང་སྙིང་ཐུབ་དོགས་པ་མེད་པ་དང་། །
གཉིས་ཀ་འདོད་ཆགས་དྲག་པོས་སྨྱོས་གྱུར་ན། །
འཁྲིག་པའི་སྐབས་སུ་ཅི་དང་ཅི་མི་བྱེད། །
ཐམས་ཅད་ཐམས་ཅད་མ་ལུས་བྱེད་པར་བྱ། །

སྐྱེས་བུ་གསུམ་པས་མཐོང་དུ་མི་རུང་ཞིང་། །
རྣ་བ་ལྡ་པས་ཐོས་སུ་མི་རུང་བའི། །
ཐུན་མོང་མ་ཡིན་གསང་བའི་འབྲེལ་བ་དག།
འཇིག་རྟེན་ཁམས་ན་སྙིང་གྲོགས་མཆོག་ཏུ་འགྱུར། །

Silently and quietly in a darkened bed,
This is not the true celebration of passion.

Thus one should know desire's sixty-four arts,
Which offer diverse flavors of bliss,
Like those of molasses, milk, and honey,
To the passionate man and woman.[93]

. 94 .

First kiss the arms and under the arms
Then slowly kiss the belly.
Becoming more intoxicated, kiss the thighs and vulva;
Draw the streams of the channels into the sea.[94]

. 95 .

Close, trusting, without worry,
When both are drunk with intense desire,
What would they not do at the time of coupling?
They do everything; they leave nothing.

Not right for a third person to see
Not right for a fifth ear to hear
Those who share the special secrets
Become best heart-friends in this world.[95]

. ༨༦ .

རིག་པའི་བུ་ཆུང་ཆགས་པའི་དབྱིངས་སུ་བརྒྱལ། །
འཇུར་བུའི་བློ་གྲོས་སྲིན་བུའི་བུ་གར་ལྡུངས། །
སྲིད་པའི་རྣམ་རྟོག་ཐུར་དུ་དྲངས་གྱུར་པས། །
དགའ་བའི་དེ་ཉིད་སྐྱེ་བོ་དག་གིས་ལྟོས། །

. ༨༧ .

དམ་པའི་འགྲོ་ལ་དག་པའི་ཆོས་ཉིད་སྟོན། །
རྨོངས་པའི་བུ་ལ་བསླུ་བའི་ཀྱལ་ཀ་བྱེད། །
མཆོན་དུ་མེད་ལ་མཚན་མའི་རྣམ་པ་ཅན། །
རང་བྱུང་དགའ་བའི་ལྷ་ལ་ཕྱག་འཚལ་ལོ། །

མ་བསྒོམ་མི་དང་བླུན་པོའི་བློ་ལ་གསལ། །
ཀུན་ལ་ཁྱོད་འགྲོགས་ཀུན་ཀྱང་ཁྱོད་ཀྱི་གྲོགས། །
ཀུན་གྱིས་མཐོང་ཞིང་སུ་ཡིས་མི་ཤེས་པ། །
རང་བྱུང་དགའ་བའི་ལྷ་ལ་ཕྱག་འཚལ་ལོ། །

ཀུན་རྫོབ་གོས་མེད་ནམ་མཁའི་གར་མཁན་མ། །
ཁ་དོག་དབྱིབས་མེད་དགུ་འགྱུར་འཕྲུལ་གྱི་གཟུགས། །
སྨྱོང་ལ་མི་ཟིན་རིག་པའི་སྐར་མདའ་འཕེན། །
རང་བྱུང་དགའ་བའི་ལྷ་ལ་ཕྱག་འཚལ་ལོ། །

གང་དུ་སྣ་ཚོགས་སྤྲོས་པའི་འཇའ་འོད་ཐིམ། །
གང་དུ་སྒྱུ་མའི་རྒྱ་མཚོ་རླབས་དང་བྲལ། །
གང་དུ་གཡོ་བའི་ཡིད་ཀྱང་མི་གཡོ་བ། །
རང་བྱུང་བདེ་བ་ཆེ་ལ་ཕྱག་འཚལ་ལོ། །

སངས་རྒྱས་སྤྱན་གྱིས་འཇུམ་པ་མེད་པར་གཟིགས། །
མང་ཐོས་སྐྱེ་བོས་སྨྲ་བ་བཅད་ཅིང་སྨྱོང་། །

. 96 .

The small child of awareness swoons in the sphere of desire;
The tangled intellect falls into a wormhole.
Drawing lustful thoughts down;
O beings, see pleasure's true nature.[96]

. 97 .

To excellent beings, you display the nature of reality
To benighted children, you play tricks
Indefinable, you have defining marks
I bow down to the god of self-arisen pleasure.

You appear to nonmeditators and to the mind of a fool,
You befriend all and all are your friend.
Seen by everyone, understood by no one,
I bow down to the god of self-arisen pleasure.

Dancer in the sky, unclothed by convention,
Magical forms, all without color or shape,
Casting the meteor of awareness, glimpsed but not grasped,
I bow down to the god of self-arisen pleasure.

Where the rainbow of diverse emanations dissolves,
Where the ocean of illusion is free from waves,
Where even the wavering mind does not waver.
I bow down to self-arisen great bliss.

The eyes of the Buddha see without blinking,
The learned know it by severing speech,

འཛིན་མེད་བློ་ཡིས་སྤྲོས་མེད་ཚུལ་དུ་མཇལ། །
རང་བྱུང་བདེ་བའི་དབྱིངས་ལ་ཕྱག་འཚལ་ལོ། །

. ༤༨ .

སྤྱང་ཀི་ཤ་ཟན་རི་བོང་རྩྭ་ཟན་གཉིས། །
ཟས་ཀྱི་དོན་དུ་གྲོས་ཁ་བསྡུར་བ་ལས། །
རེ་ཞིག་རང་རིགས་མཐུན་པའི་འཁོར་ནང་དུ། །
རང་རང་སོ་སོའི་སྤྱོད་པ་བསྐྱང་བ་ལེགས། །

འབྲོག་པ་རྣམས་ལ་ཕག་ཤ་ཟ་བ་དང་། །
གྲོང་པ་རྣམས་ལ་མར་ཁུ་འཐུང་བ་སོགས། །
མི་འདོད་ནན་གྱིས་བསྐུལ་བའི་དོན་ཀྱང་མེད། །
འདོད་ན་བཙན་གྱིས་འགོག་པའི་དོན་ཀྱང་མེད། །

བཟང་ངན་གཙང་བཙོག་རང་གི་རང་འདོད་ཙམ། །
རང་འདོད་བྱ་བ་རྟག་ཏུ་བརྗེས་ནས་འགྲོ། །
དེ་ལ་རྩོད་ཤག་འགྱེད་པ་ཐང་རེ་ཆད། །
དེ་ཡི་རྒྱུ་མཚན་འཚོལ་བ་ཉིན་རེ་མོངས། །

བྱིས་པའི་དུས་ནས་རྒྱས་ཤིང་འཕོག་པའི་བར། །
སེམས་ཀྱི་འཁྱེར་སོ་ཇི་ཙམ་བརྗེས་གྱུར་པ། །
རང་གིས་མྱོང་བས་དཔྱད་ན་ཤེས་ནུས་པས། །
ད་ལྟའི་འཆར་སྣ་འདི་ལ་ཡིད་བརྟན་ཅི། །

སྐབས་འགར་ལྷ་མོ་མཐོང་ཡང་ཞེན་ལོག་འབྱུང་། །
སྐབས་འགར་རྒན་མོ་མཐོང་ཡང་ཆགས་པ་སྐྱེ། །
འདི་ཡིན་འཁྲོ་ལ་དེ་མིན་གཞན་ཞིག་འོང་། །
སེམས་ཀྱིས་བསླུས་པ་གྲངས་ཀྱིས་ག་ལ་ཆོད། །

དེ་ལྟར་ལེགས་པར་གོ་ནས་ཡི་ཆད་དེ། །
གཏད་སོ་ཀུན་གྱི་རྩ་བ་ཞིག་གྱུར་པ། །

The ungrasping mind meets it, without concepts.
I bow down to the sphere of self-arisen bliss.[97]

. 98 .

The meat-eating wolf, the grass-eating rabbit,
Rather than discussing the nature of food,
It is best if they kept to their own ways for a while,
Within the circle of their own kind.

Making nomads eat pork,
Making villagers drink melted butter.
If they don't like it, there is no point insisting;
If they do, there is no point in stopping them.

Good and bad, clean and dirty, these are just one's own opinions.
And what one thinks goes on changing.
To keep debating will just bring fatigue.
To search for reasons will just bring trouble.

Our attitudes change so much
From childhood to when we are old and decrepit.
Analyze your own experience and you know this.
How can you have confidence in today's thoughts?

Sometimes, seeing a goddess is revolting.
Sometimes, seeing an old woman is arousing.
Thinking, "This is it," something else comes along.
How can the deceptions of the mind be counted?

Having understood well and become weary,
When the root of all conceptions is destroyed,

དེ་ནི་བདེ་བའི་ངལ་གསོ་ཆེན་པོ་སྟེ། །
མིང་གི་རྣམ་གྲངས་གཞན་ན་ཐར་པར་བརྗོད། །

. ༤༤ .

བདག་ནི་ངོ་ཚ་ཆུང་ཞིང་མོ་དད་ཆེ། །
ངན་པ་འདམས་ཤིང་བཟང་པོ་འདོར་བའི་རིགས། །
སྡོམ་པའི་མགོ་བོ་སྔོན་ནས་མེད་མོད་ཀྱང་། །
བརྫུ་ཡི་རྒྱུ་མ་ཉེ་དུས་འདི་ཙ་ཆད། །

ཆུ་ཡི་ཉ་མོའི་ལག་ལེན་ཆུ་ལ་ཟབ། །
གང་གིས་སྤྱོད་པ་དེ་ལ་རྒྱུས་སུ་ཆེ། །
དེ་ལྟར་བསམ་ནས་རང་གི་བགོ་སྐལ་གྱི། །
བསྟན་བཅོས་འདི་ཉིད་འབད་པ་ཆེན་པོས་བྲིས། །

དགེ་སློང་རྣམས་ཀྱིས་སྨད་ཀྱང་མི་ཙང་མེད། །
སྔགས་པ་རྣམས་ཀྱིས་བསྟོད་ཀྱང་མི་ཚོག་མེད། །
རྒན་པོ་ཀླུ་རྒྱལ་འབུམ་ལ་དོན་ཆུང་དང་། །
ཁྲི་ལི་བསོད་ནམས་ཐར་ལ་དོན་ཆེན་ཡིན། །

རྩོམ་པ་པོ་ནི་དགེ་འདུན་ཆོས་འཕེལ་ཡིན། །
བརྩམས་པའི་ཡུལ་ནི་གྲོང་ཁྱེར་བཅོམ་བརླག་ཡིན། །
དཀའ་བའི་གཞུང་བཤད་བྲམ་ཟེ་རྒན་པོས་ཞུས། །
སྒྲོང་བའི་དམར་ཁྲིད་ཁ་ཆེའི་བུ་མོས་བཏབ། །

བཤད་པའི་རྩ་བ་རྒྱ་གར་གཞུང་ལ་གཏུགས། །
གོ་སླའི་ཚིགས་བཅད་བོད་ཀྱི་ལུགས་སུ་བསྡེབས། །
དེ་ཕྱིར་མ་ཚང་མེད་པའི་རྒྱུ་ཚོགས་ལས། །
ཕུན་ཚོགས་འབྲས་བུ་ངེས་པར་འབྱུང་ངམ་སྙམ། །

མི་ཕམ་བཙུན་པས་གསན་ནས་བྲིས་པ་དང་། །
ཆོས་འཕེལ་འཆལ་པོས་མྱོང་ནས་བྲིས་པ་གཉིས། །

That is the great relaxation of bliss.
Another word for it is liberation.[98]

. 99 .

With little shame in myself and great faith in women
I am the kind who chooses the bad and discards the good.
Although I have not had the vows in my head for some time
The guts of pretense were destroyed only recently.

The customs of river fish are deep in the water;
What one has experienced is most familiar.
With this in mind, it was my lot
To strive to write this treatise.

If monks condemn it, that's not untoward,
If tāntrikas praise it, that's not unfitting.
To the old man, its meaning is small;
To the young man, its meaning is great.

The author is Gendun Chopel,
The place it was written is the city of Mathurā,
The difficult texts were explained by an old Brahmin,
The practical lessons were given by a Muslim girl.

The explanation is rooted in the Indian treatises;
The verses are arranged in Tibetan style, easy to understand.
Thus, from causes cumulated completely,
I feel a marvelous fruit is certain to appear.

The monk Mi pham wrote from reading.
The wanton Chopel wrote from experience.

བྱིན་རླབས་གནད་ཀྱི་ཚན་ཁ་མི་འདྲ་བ། །
ཆགས་ལྡན་པོ་མོས་ཉམས་སུ་བླངས་ན་ཤེས། །

འོན་ཀྱང་ཆགས་བྲལ་སྣང་ངོར་མང་བ་དང་། །
ཆགས་ལྡན་སྐྱེས་བུའི་སྣང་ངོར་ཅུང་བ་སོགས། །
འདི་ལ་ལྷག་ཆད་ནོར་བའི་སྐྱོན་མཆིས་ན། །
མི་འཆབ་མི་སྦེད་སྙིང་ནས་མཐོལ་ཞིང་བཤགས། །

ཚུལ་ལྡན་གྲོགས་ཀྱི་འགྲོ་ལུགས་ཞིག་པ་དང་། །
བརྫུ་བག་ཅན་གྱི་སྤྲུམ་མདོག་ཤོར་བ་སོགས། །
རང་རང་སོ་སོའི་ཉེས་པ་གང་ཡིན་དག།
ཉམས་ཆུང་མི་ཡི་མགོ་བོར་མ་འགེལ་ཅིག།

དགེ་བ་འདི་ཡིས་རིགས་མཐུན་གྲོགས་པོ་ཀུན། །
ཟ་ཟིའི་འདོད་ཆགས་སྨུག་པའི་ལམ་བཀྲལ་ཏེ། །
བཙུ་དྭག་དགའ་བའི་རི་ཡི་རྩེ་མོ་ནས། །
ཆོས་ཉིད་དོན་གྱི་ནམ་མཁའ་མཐོང་བར་ཤོག།

གཡུ་སྒྲོན་གཙྪ་ཨ་ས་ལི་ལ་སོགས། །
བདག་ལ་ལུས་ཀྱིས་འབྲེལ་བའི་བུ་མོ་རྣམས། །
བདེ་ནས་བདེ་བའི་ལམ་དང་རྟེན་བརྒྱུད་དེ། །
བདེ་ཆེན་ཆོས་སྐུའི་ས་ལ་སླེབས་པར་ཤོག།

ཡངས་པའི་ས་ལ་སྤྱོད་པའི་ཉམ་ཆུང་ཀུན། །
བརྩེ་མེད་ཁྲིམས་ཀྱི་དོང་ལས་མདོན་ཐར་ཏེ། །
མཁོ་ཞིང་འོས་པའི་མནོག་ཆུང་ལོངས་སྤྱོད་ལ། །
ཐུན་མོང་རང་དབང་ཉིད་དུ་སྤྱོད་ནུས་ཤོག།

The difference in the power of their blessings
A passionate man and woman will know through practice.

Yet if there are faults of excess or deficiency here,
Being too much for those without desire,
Being too little for the passionate,
I confess it from my heart, concealing or hiding nothing.

Do not lay on a lowly person [like me]
Whatever your own faults might be:
Destroying the ways of monastic friends and
Debunking pretense and deceit.

By this virtue, may all like-minded friends
Cross the dark road of vague desires
And see the sky of the meaning of reality
From the summit of Sixteen Pleasures Peak.

Yudön, Gangā, Asali, and the others,
The women who joined with my body,
May they persist on the path, from bliss to bliss
To arrive at great bliss, the place of the dharmakāya.

May all humble people who live on the broad earth
Be delivered from the pit of merciless laws
And be able to indulge, with freedom,
In common enjoyments, so useful and right.[99]

English Compositions

. 100 .

Look at God by two small eyes
Listen to him by two small ears
Serve him by two small hands
Go to the church by two small feet
Tell the truth by a small tongue
Be loved by a small heart
Praise God for ever and pray to him.[100]

. 101 .

Manassarowar

In the times now long forgotten
In the night of other ages,
When things were not as they now are
Lay the earth a lifeless body,
Cold and hard and all unyielding,
Like a maid in dreamless slumber,
Untouched by life's budding springmood,
Ere the glow of sunrise calls her.
          And the sky looked down and saw her.
Gently then in stealth descending,
In the rose of early twilight
Stooped and kissed her in her slumber.
And behold her young heart heaving,
Throbbed her pulse, her eyelids opened
And those eyes, all filled with wonder

Shed the hot tears of her being.
Thus was born this Lake Himalayan,
Mother of the holy Ganga.

II

Mountain-wave, mystic and dreamy,
By thy shore does stand a maiden
And the rhythm of thy water
Blends into her burning bosom,
Stands she motionless and gazing,
Knows not where her flocks are straying.

The young hunter aims his arrow,
And, behold, he sees thy water,
And no more sees he the roebuck
Slacks the bowstring, flees the quarry.

When the sun in golden glory
Sheds his aureole o'er thy surface,—
Standst thou like the shrine *Chamcapa*
But the white dreamrays of moon-light
Veil thee in a garb of silver,
In the robe of Melareppa.[101]

. 102 .

Oh Where?

A city there is which lone does stand
In ruins mid bamboo trees
Hot blows the burning desert sand

Where dry shrubs sigh on the thirsting land
Where monkeys cry, and with these
Joins the shrill cry of the jungle cock
Where a maiden drives her scattered flock
To the tune of an ancient lay.
Where an ox-cart moves on its lazy way
And halts for shade neath a jutting rock;
Oh, City, where is the day,
When on thy golden Throne sat Kings
Of a mighty name and a mighty race,
Who held the Sceptre high in this place?
Hark, heareth thou Time's fleet wings?[102]

. 103 .

Repkong

My feet are wandering neath alien stars,
My native land,—the road is far and long.
Yet the same light of Venus and Mars
Falls on the small green valley of Repkong.

Repkong,—I left thee and my heart behind,
My boyhood's dusty plays,—in far Tibet.
Karma, that restless stallion made of wind,
In tossing me; where will it land me yet?

Like autumn cloud I float, soon, there, soon here,
I know not what the fleeting moons may bring.
Here in this land of roses, fair Cashmere,
My years are closing round me like a ring,

Fate sternly sits at Destiny's hard loom
And irrevoked her tangled pattern weaves
The winds are blowing round my father's tomb
And I but dream of those still summer eves,
When—child—I listened to my mother's voice,
Whose stories made my youthful heart rejoice.

So far, so far I may not see those graves,
Ah, friend, these separation pangs are sore.
My heart is thrown upon the ocean waves
Where shall at last I reach a peaceful shore?

I've drunk of holy Ganges glistening wave,
I've sat beneath the sacred Bodhi tree,
Whose leaves the wanderer's weary spirit lave.
Thou sacred land of Ind, I honour thee,
But, oh, that little valley of Repkong,
The sylvan brook which flows that vale along.[103]

. 104 .

Melareppa's Reply

The earth and the sky held counsel one night,
And called their messengers from northern height.
And came they, the stormfiends, the bleak and the cold,
They, who the stormwinds in grim fingers hold.

They swept o'er the earth, and then they called forth
That glist'ning maid from the far Polar North
In white trailing robe, the Queen of the Snow
And she sent her flutt'ring plumed children below

And downward they flew in wild, whirling showers,
While in black masses hung the threat'ning sky.
Some were like large cruel sharp-stinging flowers
Some pierced his chest with a fierce-cutting eye.

Thus stormfiends, snow and icy frost blending,
Came cold and sharply upon him descending.
On his half nude from these shapes did alight
And tried with his single thin garment to fight.

But, Melareppa, the Snow-mountain's child,
Feared not their onslaughts, so cruel and wild.
Though they attacked him most fiercely and grim,
He only smiled,—they had no power over him.[104]

Abbreviations

Collected Works *'Dzam gling rig pa'i dpa' bo mkhas dbang dge 'dun chos 'phel gyi gsung 'bum*, 5 vols. (Hong Kong: Zhang kang gyi ling dpe skrun khang, 2006).

Chos grags *Dge bshes chos kyi grags pas brtsams pa'i brda dag ming tshig gsal ba; Tibetan dictionary by Geshe Chhosdag* (Delhi: Gangs chung sprul sku, 1967).

Dhongthog T. G. Dhongthog, *Dge 'dun chos 'phel gyi gsung rtsom*, 3 vols. (Bir, India: Dzongsar Institute, 1991).

Gsar rnyed Rdo rje rgyal, ed., *Mkhas dbang dge 'dun chos 'phel gyi gsar rnyed gsung rtsom* (Xining: Mtsho sngon mi rigs par khang, 2002).

Hor khang Hor khang bsod nams dpal 'bar, ed., *Dge 'dun chos 'phel gyi gsung rtsom*, 3 vols. (Gangs can rig mdzod 10–12) (Lhasa: Bod ljongs bod yig dpe rnying dpe skrun khang, 1990).

Phyogs sgrig Bsod nams don grub et al., eds., *Mkhas dbang dge 'dun chos 'phel gyi gsung rtsom phyogs sgrig* (Chengdu: Si khron mi rigs dpe skrun khang, 1994).

Rnam thar Rdo rje rgyal, *'Dzam gling rig pa'i dpa' bo rdo brag dge 'dun chos 'phel gyi byung ba brjod pa bden gtam rna ba'i bcud len* (Lanzhou: Kan su'u mi rigs dpe skrun khang, 1997).

Notes

1. *Collected Works* 5:159–60; Hor khang 11, pp. 393–95, where the poem is entitled "Song Sent to Hor khang from Prison."
2. *Collected Works* 5:170; Hor khang 11, p. 403, where the poem is entitled "In Praise of Tārā."
3. *Collected Works* 5:171–73; Hor khang 11, pp. 403–6, where the poem is entitled "Advice on the Practice of the Essential Sacred Dharma." The colophon says, "This was written by the cosmopolitan Dge 'dun chos 'phel for Sgrol ma g.yang 'dzoms, who has turned toward the essential dharma." Sgrol ma g.yang 'dzoms (1884–1965?) was a woman from Khams who married a British sergeant named William Henry Luff. They lived in an eleven-room house in Darjeeling, where she remained after his death in 1942 or 1943. Many prominent Tibetan lamas and scholars were guests in her house, including Gendun Chopel, who wrote this poem and painted a thangka of Vaiśrāvana, the god of wealth, during a visit to Darjeeling, probably in the early 1940s.
4. *Collected Works* 5:138; Hor khang 11, p. 411.
5. *Collected Works* 5:138–39; Hor khang 11, p. 412.
6. *Collected Works* vol. 5:139; Hor khang 11, pp. 412–13.
7. *Collected Works* 4:257; Hor khang 12, p. 313.
8. *Collected Works* 4:284; Hor khang 12, pp. 342–43.
9. *Collected Works* 4:290; Hor khang 12, p. 350.
10. *Collected Works* 2:72; Hor khang 10, p. 89.
11. *Collected Works* 2:155; Hor khang 10, p. 191.
12. *Collected Works* 2:209; Hor khang 10, pp. 257–58.
13. *Collected Works* 4:140; Hor khang 11, p. 379.
14. *Chos grags*, p. 1.
15. *Collected Works* 5:281–82; Hor khang 12, p. 537 and foldout final page, where the poem is entitled, "Auspicious Circle Offered to the Throne Holder of Smin gling."
16. *Rnam thar*, pp. 14–15.
17. *Rnam thar*, pp. 20–21. After leaving Labrang Monastery and before departing

from Lhasa, Gendun Chopel returned to his home village to visit his mother and sister. While there, he read the autobiography of the great nineteenth century Nyingma lama Zhabs dkar tshogs drug rang grol (1781–1851), whose hermitage was located at the monastery where Gendun Chopel first studied. He composed this poem of praise after reading the text. There is a notation indicating that he wrote this poem on "25-8-26," although it is unclear whether the day and month refer to the Tibetan or the European calendar.

18. *Rnam thar*, p. 25. During his time as a monk in Lhasa, Gendun Chopel became a favorite of Pha bong kha pa (1878–1943), the most powerful monk in the Geluk sect during the first half of the twentieth century. Gendun Chopel painted thangkas for him, writing this poem on the back of one of them. It is based on Pha bong kha pa's personal name, Byams pa bstan 'dzin 'phrin las rgya mtsho, literally "Kindness, Upholder of the Teaching, Deeds, Ocean," which appears in order in the four lines of the poem.
19. *Rnam thar*, p. 94.
20. *Rnam thar*, p. 135. Śuddhodana is the Buddha's father.
21. *Rnam thar*, p. 135. The temple here is the Jo khang in Lhasa.
22. *Collected Works* 2:237; Hor khang 10, p. 292.
23. *Collected Works* 5:148; the first stanza also occurs at Hor khang 11, p. 409.
24. *Collected Works* 2:70; Hor khang 10, p. 87. Gendun Chopel is being sarcastic here, mocking those Tibetan authors who claim to find prophecies concerning Tibet by misreading Indian scriptures.
25. Dhongthog 2:352–53.
26. *Collected Works* 4:1; Hor khang 11, p. 273. This and the remaining poems in this section appear in Gendun Chopel's controversial essay on Madhyamaka philosophy, *The Adornment for Nāgārjuna's Thought* (*Klu sgrub dgongs rgyan*). For a translation and study of that text, with comments on these poems, see Donald S. Lopez Jr., *The Madman's Middle Way: Reflections on Reality of the Tibetan Monk Gendun Chopel* (Chicago: University of Chicago Press, 2005). In the text, this poem, which opens *The Adornment for Nāgārjuna's Thought*, continues for two more stanzas, which, according to Gendun Chopel's friend Rak ra bkras mthong, were not composed by Gendun Chopel but were added by one of his students, Zla ba bzang po.

> Eye of the world, displaying subtlety, without error, through your aspiration to the path of liberation,
> Source of the ambrosia of excellent virtue and soothing peace,
> The assembled philosophers ever respect you without waxing or waning, saying,
> "This is the lord of the dharma, supreme lion of speakers."

From the maṇḍala of the sun of your wisdom in Samantabhadra's sky,
In the lotus garden of my heart's meager knowledge, innate or acquired,
[Grows] the glorious smiling stamen of eloquence, surrounded by a thousand rays of reasoning.
May the bees of scholars of the three realms enjoy the sweet honey of the true transmission.

27. *Collected Works* 4:16; Hor khang 11, p. 292.
28. *Collected Works* 4:19–22; Hor khang 11, pp. 297–301.
29. *Collected Works* 4:32; Hor khang 11, p. 315.
30. *Collected Works* 4:78–79; Hor khang 11, pp. 374–75.
31. *Collected Works* 5:153–54. Hor khang 11, pp. 389–90, where it is entitled, "Alphabetical Poem Sent to Labrang." In 1927, Gendun Chopel left the monastery of Labrang, where he had spent as many as seven years (the precise length of his time there is unknown). The reasons for his departure are not known; everything ranging from criticizing the monastery's textbooks to making mechanical toys has been mentioned. Here, he indicates that he studied other textbooks, the famous "collected topics" (*bsdus grwa*) of Rwa stod and Bse. However, there was a rumor that his expulsion had been ordered by Gnas chung, the wrathful protector deity of the monastery. Gendun Chopel was clearly incensed by this rumor and wrote this poem, which he sent back to the monastery. At the end, he refers to himself as "the sophist Saṃghadharma." He was accused by some at the monastery of being a sophist (*tha snyad pa*), that is, someone who could debate skillfully but had little understanding of the deeper meaning. Saṃghadharma is the Sanskrit version of the first three syllables of his name.
32. *Collected Works* 5:161–64; Hor khang 11, pp. 395–99, where it is entitled, "Song Remembering Impermanence." There are two versions of this famous poem. The first appeared in 1980 in Bkras mthong thub bstan chos dar, *Dge 'dun chos 'phel gyi lo rgyus* (Dharamsala: Library of Tibetan Works and Archives, 1980), pp. 71–74. It is simply entitled "Song" (*gsung mgur*). Another version of the same poem appeared in 1990 in Gendun Chopel's collected writings, under the title "Mi rtag pa dran pa'i gsung mgur," or "Song Remembering Impermanence," in Hor khang 11 (pp. 395–99, reprinted in *Collected Works* 5:161–64). There are a significant number of differences between the poems, some of which cannot be attributed simply to scribal error, illegible calligraphy, or the homophony of Tibetan. The most significant of these differences is the omission of the stanza about the lion and the dog from the 1990 version. In addition, the 1980 version reads, "The way I used to think about meaningful [*don chen*] things." The 1990 version reads, "The way I used to think about meaningless [*don med*] things." The second stanza of the 1980 version mentions the *kang lang skad*, perhaps

"the voice of the Kalantaka bird," while the 1990 version has *rkang gling skad*, "the voice of the thighbone trumpet." There are some two dozen differences between the two poems, enough to suggest that they are indeed two distinct versions of the poem. Their chronology, whether they were both written and edited by Gendun Chopel, and which he considered the "final" version, are all unknown.

Despite the temptation to produce a translation that culls the "preferable" reading from the two versions of the poem, I have translated the 1990 (and more recent *Collected Works*) version here, including the stanza about the lion and the dog to indicate where this passage falls in the 1980 version. According to Gendun Chopel's friend Rak ra bkras mthong, that stanza refers to the time spent working with George Roerich on the *Blue Annals*.

Two stanzas—one stanza that appears in both poems (with yet further variants) and the stanza about the lion and the dog—appear as "Fragment Six" (*thor bu drug pa*) in the same volume of the *Collected Works*, p. 136 (Hor khang, pp. 409–10).

33. *Collected Works* 5:165–67; Hor khang 11, pp. 399–401, where it is entitled, "Song of the Realization of the Futility of Meeting and Parting." When Gendun Chopel departed for Lhasa in 1927, he was accompanied by an uncle and his son, Gendun Chopel's cousin. The three parted ways in Lhasa, with the uncle becoming a meditator and the cousin working odd jobs to support Gendun Chopel and his father. Several years after arriving in Lhasa, the cousin was killed in an accident. Gendun Chopel wrote this poem about the death of his childhood friend.
34. *Collected Works* 5:136; Hor khang 11, p. 409.
35. *Collected Works* 5:136–37; Hor khang 11, pp. 410–11.
36. *Collected Works* 4:138; Hor khang 11, p. 269. This is the first of two colophons to his translation of the *Dhammapada* from Pāli into Tibetan.
37. *Collected Works* 4:139; Hor khang 11, p. 270. This is the second colophon to his translation of the *Dhammapada*, added when the blocks were carved in Sikkim in 1945.
38. *Collected Works* 3:92; Hor khang 11, p. 73. This poem was written in Sri Lanka, describing his meeting with the Theravāda monks of the island after he himself had renounced his monk's vows.
39. *Collected Works* 3:97; Hor khang 11, pp. 81–82.
40. *Collected Works* 1:179–80 and 3:102; Hor khang 12, p. 224 and 11, p. 87. In the second occurrence in each case, the second line reads *tho co'i 'ol tshod* rather than *rlom pa'i 'ol tshod*, "foolishly" rather than "with pride."
41. *Collected Works* 3:173; Hor khang 11, p. 175.
42. *Collected Works* 3:181–82; Hor khang 11, pp. 184–86. This is the colophon to

Gendun Chopel's major work, *The Golden Chronicle* (*Gser gyi thang ma*), which he completed in Sri Lanka and sent to Tibet in 1941.

43. *Chos grags*, p. 1. This poem appears in the famous Tibetan dictionary compiled by Gendun Chopel's friend, the Mongolian scholar Geshe Chos grags. Although this poem is officially attributed to him, many feel that it was in fact written by Gendun Chopel.

44. From the unpublished poems distributed at the Latse Conference, New York (November 7–9, 2003), with portions in *Rnam thar*, pp. 54, 55, 70. The unpublished version contains the colophon, "This was written under a palm tree not far from the Vishnu temple of Jaganatha [at a place] that is part of the land of Kalinga, a region where one can see the ocean that is like the sky." In the sixth stanza, the commentaries to Śāntideva's *Bodhicaryāvatāra* are presumably those of Chu mig pa Seng ge dpal (ca. 1200–70) and perhaps one by Yang dgon pa Rgyal mtshan dpal (1213–1258), which Gendun Chopel may have located during his visit to Snar thang Monastery in 1938. It was there that he met the fifth 'Jam dbyangs bzhad pa (1916–1947), whom he refers to in the fifth stanza. The poem was given to Rdo rje rgyal by Akhu Blo bzang bsam gtan.

45. *Rnam thar*, p. 57.

46. *Rnam thar*, p. 65.

47. *Rnam thar*, p 65. Utpalavarṇā was a famous female disciple of the Buddha who joined the order of nuns and achieved liberation from rebirth. She was the first to greet him when he descended from the Heaven of the Thirty-Three, where he had gone to teach the dharma to his mother, who had been reborn as a god.

48. *Me long* 9, nos. 7–8, January 2, 1938, p. 13. End of essay "Dbu can las dbu med rang byung du grub pa."

49. *Collected Works* 5:87. This poem concludes a letter (5:82–87) that Hor khang received from Gendun Chopel on the thirtieth day of the eleventh month of the Fire Dog Year (hence early 1947). In the letter, written from prison, Gendun Chopel discusses his interrogation, saying that he put forward his work on the history of Tibet as evidence of his loyalty. He is very concerned that the history be completed and published. Should he die before the book is finished, he provides a poem for Hor khang to place at the end of the unfinished manuscript. This is poem 87. Most of the letter is taken up with a discussion of various historical inscriptions. At the conclusion of the letter, Gendun Chopel mentions that he has transcribed an ancient Tibetan poem that he had committed to memory. He asks that this poem be framed in glass after his death. He then exhorts Hor khang to continue to work on the history, which Hor khang would eventually publish as the *White Annals* (*Deb ther dkar po*). The letter concludes with this poem, addressed to Hor khang.

The following is the poem that Gendun Chopel had committed to memory.

It appears in his collected works with the title "Btson nas gnang ba'i btsan po khri gtsug lde btsan gyi mgur tshig skad gsar bcad du bcos pa" (*Collected Works* 5:88–89), "Sent from Prison, A Song of King Khri gtsug lde btsan, Composed in Modern Language." It is presumably some version of an ancient Tibetan poem discovered at Dunhuang, which Gendun Chopel might have been shown by Jacques Bacot in India. Gendun Chopel would have updated the language, hence the term "modern language."

From the high heaven of the exalted gods
Above the seven levels of the azure sky,
The divine son of gods, the lord of men,
Did not come to just any land.
This land of Zal mo, with its fence of snows,
Its mountain ranges lofty, its ground pure;
Different and better than all other places,
Thus, the son of gods came to this land of Tibet.
In this savage place, the kingdom of the red-faced,
There were many who said, "I am the great."
But from that time, all the minor kingdoms
United under the one divine emperor.
Downstream where the great and small rivers flow,
Downstream from the upper waters of the Tsang po,
At a place in China, in a land far away,
The Chinese general Kwag lo pong [said]
"I am the friend of the lord of Tibet.
I heard of you two or three years ago.
Your mind is open and your intelligence great.
You are courageous, a general skilled with the enemy.
In China, foes pretend to be friends;
Disillusioned, I have turned away.
As a suffering child seeks protection from its father,
I seek protection from the divine prince of Tibet.
Pull the fortress of mighty China to the ground;
Lead the Chinese subjects to Tibet.
Gather the kingdom of China and its armies
Into the royal land of Tibet, the kingdom of Pur.
Two or three years before, a Chinese general,
Failing to defeat you, turned the point
Of his sharp weapon toward Tibet.

So you, the divine son, rose as an enemy against me.
When I see you these days,
We have become master and servant.
If the kind lord is not abandoned by his subject,
How can the lord abandon his humble subject?
If you are near me, I will come nearer,
The blue sky is close to the gods.
If you rely on me, I will be reliant for you,
Like the snow relies on the mountain spirits.
I am bound by the command of the divine prince of Tibet;
Words spoken in the past will not be changed in the future.
The heart of the divine prince of Tibet is good;
The kindness of the past will not be forgotten in the future.
The prince is like the blue sky, and La bong is like the earth,
It is the emissary Cung kwag who brings them together
Through a parting in the dark mists of the clouds.
The blue sky seen above is pleased;
The earth seen below is pleased.
The returning guest was not received from the front;
The departing friend was not sent off from behind.
Songs of joy were sung, dances were danced.
How splendid the good fortune gathered in this circle."
Ki bswo bswo lha rgyal lo

50. *Collected Works* 2:3–4; Hor khang 10, p. 6.
51. From the unpublished poems distributed at the Latse Conference, New York (November 7–9, 2003). This poem is said to have been recited extemporaneously by Gendun Chopel when he was asked to compose his autobiography. The poem was given to Rdo rje rgyal by Byams pa 'phrin las.
52. *Rnam thar*, p. 72.
53. *Collected Works* 5:155–56; Hor khang 11, pp. 390–92, where it is entitled, "Alphabetical Poem, Story of a Household Priest."
54. *Collected Works* 5:157–58; Hor khang 11, pp. 392–93; also *Me long* 8, no. 8, October 16, 1936. It is entitled there, "Alphabetical Poem Expressed Sincerely in the Common Language."
55. *Collected Works* 5:168–69; Hor khang 11, pp. 401–02, where it is entitled, "Observations of a Cosmopolitan." Chandra Shamsher Jung Bahadur Rana (1863–1929; reigned. 1901–29) was the fifth prime minister of Nepal during the Rana period.

56. *Collected Works* 5:132–33; Hor khang 11, pp. 406–07.
57. *Collected Works* 5:133–35; Hor khang 11, pp. 407–08. The first, second, fourth, and fifth stanzas occur also in Dhongthog, 2:356; the third stanza occurs in Dhongthog, 2:353.
58. *Collected Works* 5:135; Hor khang 11, pp. 408–09. See variant in *Collected Works* 2:220 and Hor khang 10, pp. 270–71. The first four lines are said to have been found written on the mattress in Gendun Chopel's prison cell upon his release.
59. *Collected Works* 5:149, where it is entitled "A Section from the Play Śakuntalā." The final two stanzas (which appear also at Hor khang 11, p. 411) seem to describe the experience of watching a motion picture. The "golden-haired monkeys" are the British.
60. *Collected Works* 4:139; Hor khang 11, p. 270; variant *Collected Works* 2:207 and Hor khang 10, p. 255, with the first line reading, "Although the door to the treasury of wondrous words has been opened."
61. *Collected Works* 5:151–52; *Gsar rnyed*, pp. 287–88, where it is entitled, "Alphabetical Poem Offered to Babu Tharchin." This poem was written for Dorje Tharchin (1890–1976), founder and editor of *Me long*, the Tibetan-language newspaper, published in Kalimpong. He was also a prominent Tibetan Christian, hence the Christian themes of the poem. Gendun Chopel was a regular contributor to *Me long*. This poem first appeared on the front page of *Me long* 8, no. 10, January 13, 1937, with the title, "Alphabetical Poem Received from a Learned Man." There are significant variants between the original *Me long* version and the more recently published version; the *Me long* version is translated here. In the first line, the word *perfect* is *mthar phyin* in Tibetan, and thus the line can also be read, "To my friend Tharchin."
62. *Collected Works* 5:130–32; *Gsar rnyed*, pp. 317–19, where it is entitled, "On the Composition of Poetry."
63. *Collected Works* 5:140–42; *Gsar rnyed*, pp. 320–22, where it is entitled, "Poem Composed in India."
64. *Collected Works* 5:143–46; *Gsar rnyed*, pp. 323–327, where it is entitled, "Song Offered to Bla brang."
65. *Collected Works* 5:148; *Phyogs sgrig*, p. 419.
66. *Phyogs sgrig*, p. 420; *Rnam thar*, p. 62.
67. *Collected Works* 2:1–2; Hor khang 10, pp. 3–4. This poem opens *The Golden Chronicle*.
68. *Collected Works* 2:66; Hor khang 10, p. 82.
69. *Collected Works* 2:271; Hor khang 10, p. 335.
70. *Collected Works* 3:110; Hor khang 11, p. 97.
71. *Collected Works* 3:151; Hor khang 11, pp. 147–48.

72. *Collected Works* 3:162; Hor khang 11, pp. 161–62.
73. *Collected Works* 4:145; Hor khang 11, p. 385.
74. From the unpublished poems distributed at the Latse Conference, New York (November 7–9, 2003). The poem was given to Rdo rje rgyal by La mo Yongs 'dzin.
75. Recorded by Heather Stoddard in 2003.
76. *Rnam thar*, p. 16.
77. *Rnam thar*, pp. 66–67.
78. *Me long* 9, no. 12, May 30, 1938, front page. It carries the title, "Listen to the Lute of the Cool Realm." This poem is filled with astrological symbolism concerning the period of the death of the Thirteenth Dalai Lama and the discovery of the Fourteenth Dalai Lama. It alludes specifically to Reting (Rwa sgreng) Rinpoche, the regent at that time.
79. *Me long* 12, no. 9, April 1944, p. 12. The poem appeared in *Me long* near the end of the Second World War.
80. *Collected Works* 2:39–40.
81. *Chos grags*, pp. 781–82. This is the poem that concludes the Tibetan dictionary compiled by the Mongolian scholar Geshe Chos grags. Although officially attributed to Geshe Chos grags, many feel it was composed by Gendun Chopel.
82. *Collected Works* 1:168; Hor khang 12, pp. 209–10. The four domains are Khrims kyi sde, Dmag gi sde, Dpal gi sde, Mnga' thang gi sde.
83. *Collected Works* 1:188; Hor khang 12, 234–35. Also *Me long*, September 8, 1943, p. 3.
84. *Collected Works* 1:208; Hor khang 12, p. 259.
85. *Collected Works* 1:229; Hor khang 12, p. 284.
86. *Collected Works* 1:241; Hor khang 12, p. 299.
87. *Collected Works* 1:241; Hor khang 12, p. 299. See variant at *Rnam thar*, pp. 107–8. In a letter sent from prison, Gendun Chopel asked Hor khang to add this poem to the conclusion of the *White Annals* in the event that the work remained unfinished. See note to poem 49.
88. *Collected Works* 4:293–96; Hor khang 12, pp. 303–6. In the tenth stanza, the two goals are the welfare of oneself and others; the three times are past, present, and future; the fourfold wealth is *artha*, *kāma*, *dharma*, and *mokṣa*. A variant of this stanza is found as *Collected Works* 1:220; Hor khang 12, p. 273.
89. *Collected Works* 4:298; Hor khang 12, p. 308.
90. *Collected Works* 5:9; Dhongthog 2:276.
91. *Collected Works* 5:9; Dhongthog 2:276.
92. *Collected Works* 5:11; Dhongthog 2:278.
93. *Collected Works* 5:29; Dhongthog 2:302.
94. *Collected Works* 5:32–33; Dhongthog 2:306.

95. *Collected Works* 5:42; Dhongthog 2:319.
96. *Collected Works* 5:67; Dhongthog 2:353.
97. *Collected Works* 5:68–69; Dhongthog 2:354–55.
98. *Collected Works* 5:69–70; Dhongthog 2:356. See also poem 56. The fourth stanza also occurs at *Collected Works* 4:7 and at Hor khang 11, p. 281.
99. *Collected Works* 5:71–72; Dhongthog 2:357–59.
100. *Gsar rnyed*, front matter. The poem is dated "11-1-43" and signed "G. Chomphel, Y.M.B.A., Dorjeeling." YMBA stands for Young Men's Buddhist Association.
101. *Maha-Bodhi* (August 1941): 293.
102. *Maha-Bodhi* (August 1941): 294.
103. *Maha-Bodhi* (August 1941): 294–95.
104. *Maha-Bodhi* (August 1941): 295.

Index of First Lines